M000158320

MODERN
KOREA

Andrew Salmon

First published in Great Britain in 2014 by John Murray Learning. An Hachette UK company.

First published in US in 2014 by The McGraw-Hill Companies, Inc.

This edition published in 2014 by John Murray Learning

British Library Cataloguing in Publication Data: a catalogue record for this title is available from the British Library.

Library of Congress Catalog Card Number: on file.

Paperback ISBN 978 1 473 60125 3

eBook ISBN 978 1 473 60127 7

10 9 8 7 6 5 4 3 2 1

The publisher has used its best endeavours to ensure that any website addresses referred to in this book are correct and active at the time of going to press. However, the publisher and the author have no responsibility for the websites and can make no guarantee that a site will remain live or that the content will remain relevant, decent or appropriate.

The publisher has made every effort to mark as such all words which it believes to be trademarks. The publisher should also like to make it clear that the presence of a word in the book, whether marked or unmarked, in no way affects its legal status as a trademark.

Every reasonable effort has been made by the publisher to trace the copyright holders of material in this book. Any errors or omissions should be notified in writing to the publisher, who will endeavour to rectify the situation for any reprints and future editions.

Typeset by Cenveo® Publisher Services.

Printed and bound in Great Britain by CPI Group (UK) Ltd., Croydon, CR0 4YY.

John Murray Learning policy is to use papers that are natural, renewable and recyclable products and made from wood grown in sustainable forests. The logging and manufacturing processes are expected to conform to the environmental regulations of the country of origin.

John Murray Learning
338 Euston Road
London NW1 3BH

www.hodder.co.uk

Contents

CHINA

Hyesan
Chongjin

Kanggye

Kimchaek

Sinuiju

Hamhung

Korea
Bay

Wonsan

☆ **Pyongyang**

Nampo

100 mi

NORTH KOREA

100 km

Haeju

Taebaek
Mntns

Chuncheon

38° - - - - - - - - - - - - -

☆ **Seoul**

Gangneung

Incheon

Suwon   Wonju

Sea of
Japan
(East Sea)

Yellow
Sea (West Sea)

**SOUTH
KOREA**

Andong

Daejeon

Gunsan

Chonju

Pohang

Daegu

**Sobaek
Mtns**

Masan

Mokpo

Busan

Gwangju

Korea Strait

Yeosu

Jeju Strait

Mt *Halla*

JAPAN

*Jeju
Island*

LOW / HILLS / MOUNTAINS

▲ Map of the Korean Peninsula.

Preface: land of extremes

British historical novelist George MacDonald-Fraser reflected that the conquest of the American West took place with breathtaking speed. A child could cross the Great Plains by wagon train during the Gold Rush, then, in his dotage, watch the drama re-enacted on television. Yet, by the standards of a land on the opposite side of the Pacific – vaguely known in the nineteenth century as 'The Hermit Kingdom' – even this pace of change appears sluggish.

A Korean born in Seoul in (say) 1900 would have grown up in the twilight of Joseon, a dynasty founded a hundred years before Columbus discovered America. He would have come of age under the harsh but modernizing force of Japanese imperialism and then experienced the joy of liberation, the bitterness of division and the horror of one of the twentieth century's nastiest wars. Finally, against all expectations, he would have witnessed his nation transform itself into an industrial powerhouse and a vibrant democracy. In his nineties, he might even have visited the last king's palace. Traditionally, no Seoul building was allowed to be higher than the palace's two storeys; today it is overshadowed by high-rises. He might travel there in a locally made car and capture it on a locally made digital camera – devices that, in his youth, would have been wondrous.

Even this dramatic transformation is not the full story, for there is another Korea. In 2012 two books were published. Daniel Tudor's *Korea: The Impossible Nation* covered South Korea; Victor Cha's *The Impossible State: North Korea Past and Future* covered North Korea. Both titles are appropriate, for South Korea represents arguably the greatest national success story of the twentieth century, North Korea one of its worst failures.

The Asian renaissance is one of the mightiest trends in recent history, but, even amid this, Korea stands out. Most economies of the region enjoyed a prior economy of scale, a heritage of modernization or at least a background in global commerce. Not so Korea. The peninsula was a minnow compared to China, had neither any record of drastic modernization, as did Meiji Japan, nor any experience of colonial-era trade like Singapore or Hong Kong. This makes South Korea's 'zero-to-hero' success doubly remarkable. Meanwhile, North Korea's continued existence puzzles pundits and exasperates policymakers who have been anticipating its collapse since the 1990s. Ergo: South Korea represents against-all-odds national success; North Korea is an equally unexpected model of regime survival.

The peninsula that exploded into the world's consciousness with the 1950 war is more globally relevant than ever. South Korea is a high-tech manufacturing superpower, a central player in global trade and Asia's most dynamic pop-cultural force; its accelerated economic, political and social development provides benchmarks for developing nations. Meanwhile, nuclear-armed North Korea casts a long shadow over not just the peninsula, but also China, Japan and the Russian Far East. North-east Asia is the world's third largest zone of economic activity after Europe and North America, but is also an area of awesome strategic risk. For these reasons, Korea is relevant to parliaments, newsrooms and boardrooms, but is poorly understood. (This is partly because of its idiosyncrasies. For example, South Korean capitalism is as different from Anglo-Saxon capitalism as North Korean communism was from Russian communism.).

And a colossal challenge beckons: reunification. The perils are heart-stopping. Beijing and Washington could find themselves (again) at war; a nuclear holocaust could sweep North-east Asia. Yet the potential rewards are as huge: the dissolution of North Korea would remove a strategic *casus belli* in the region and promote further integration between China, Korea, Japan and Russia. Hence the most dramatic chapter of the Korean story may be, as yet, unwritten.

The existence of two diametrically opposed states dividing the same people underlines a standout trend of modern Korea: on this mountainous peninsula, things extend to their most distant extremes. For centuries in Korea, faction contended with faction as forces favouring orthodoxy struggled against proponents of heterodoxy, and as demands for internationalization clashed with forces favouring parochialism. In the twentieth century these paradigms were magnified by interface with international trends: Cold War confrontation, global trade and international communications. South Korea has achieved undreamed-of success by opening itself to the world. North Korea has sunk into poverty and stagnation by closing itself off, becoming (in both senses of the phrase) another 'Hermit Kingdom'.

What follows is not a comprehensive history, but an explication of key issues. As most Korea-related literature covers the North, this work concentrates on the South; Seoul is more globally relevant, and for better reasons, than Pyongyang. I hope that it provides newcomers with a solid grounding and experts with a few nuggets. From devastation to development; from human rights to atomic arms; from Samsung to Psy; this is the story of a peninsula once dubbed 'Land of Morning Calm' but which today may be better understood as 'The Land of Extremes'.

I must thank Peter Bartholomew, Bernie Cho, Choe Sang-hoon, Dr Choi Jin-wook, Sebastien Falletti, Dr Kim Jeong-noh, Kim Shin-jo, Sue Kim, Dr Andrei Lankov, Lee Hyeon-seo, Dr Lee Doo-won, Dr Tony Michell, Hank Morris, Dr Brian Myers, Robert Neff, Park So-keel, James Pearson, Ambassador Rah Yong-yil, Mark Russell, Dr Shin Se-don, Dr Yoon Jung-won and Jacco Zwetzloot for their thoughts. Thanks, especially, to Lee Chang-seop and Oh Young-jin at the *Korea Times* for publishing my column, which explores several themes contained herein; and to Mike Breen and Jack Burton for endless discussions about this ever-engaging land.

Andrew Salmon

Seoul, May 2014

1

Division and devastation

*'When whales fight,
shrimps are crushed.'*

Korean proverb

In the summer of 1950, American, British and Australian servicemen received orders to deploy urgently to the Far East in defence of a nation reeling from communist invasion. Few imagined the destruction and horror they would encounter on a battlefield few had even heard of: Korea.

▶ Twilight of the Hermit Kingdom

The Korean Peninsula lies at the crossroads of Northeast Asia: a 'shrimp' between the 'whales' of China, Japan and the Russian Far East. It is a jagged land, corrugated by ridges and mountains. Spring and autumn are fine, clear seasons, but the monsoon summers are sweltering, winters harsh and freezing. Extreme weather and rugged terrain make the peninsula a beautiful but hard land.

Korean mythic history dates back to the dawn of time; recorded history begins in the heroic age of the 'Three Kingdoms', around the first century CE. Debate continues as to how far Korean kingdoms were vassals of Chinese dynasties, but local culture was massively influenced by the Middle Kingdom. Korea imported religious, governance, educational, agricultural, medical, artistic, literary and philosophical systems including Buddhism, Confucianism, calligraphy, acupuncture and herbal medicine from China; in turn, it channelled these things to Japan. Yet, though Korea absorbed many Sinic influences, it boasted a distinct language, a bespoke alphabet, a native religion, a fine pottery tradition and an idiosyncratic cuisine.

The Three Kingdoms – Goguryeo, Baekje and Silla – were unified by Silla victory in 668 CE. Silla was succeeded by the Goryeo Dynasty (the word 'Korea' is a romanization of Goryeo), which ruled the peninsula until 1392, when it was overthrown by Joseon. 'Joseon' means 'fair morning', hence Korea would be dubbed (in a minor mistranslation) 'Land of Morning Calm'. Joseon was also branded 'The Hermit Kingdom', for in the seventeenth century it closed its borders to the outside world. Dozing behind shuttered doors, this Asian backwater, bar some diplomacy with China and Japan, was almost entirely severed from international developments. By the nineteenth century, Joseon was one of the world's longest-running dynasties, but its isolation could not last, for the age of colonization was at its apex.

Aggressive nations equipped with industrialized transport and military technologies were competing to fill the blank spaces on their maps. To the east, Japan, in one of the most remarkable national transformations in history, overturned seclusionist policies and radically modernized. As it opened an expansive eye, Tokyo's first target was obvious: the peninsula that formed a land-bridge into the Asian continent. With merchants and warriors looked down upon by Joseon's scholarly elite, the kingdom was ill-equipped to face down aggression, either economic or military. In 1876, using gunboat diplomacy, Meiji Japan prised open Korea's creaking gates. Other powers swiftly followed, exposing Joseon to modernization and internationalization.

Goggling diplomats, missionaries, businessmen and travellers discovered a time capsule – a living medieval kingdom complete with royals, scholar-aristocrats, concubines, eunuchs, peasants and slaves. Even by Victorian standards, there was nothing approaching modern administration, infrastructure or industry. Joseon's King Gojeong made some efforts at modernization. He hired foreign consultants for his customs and army and allowed foreign businessmen to establish trams, rail lines and mines. But his kingdom's strategic position made it the prize in a power game between decrepit China, imperialistic Russia and rising Japan.

In 1894 Korea's biggest-ever peasant rebellion, the Donghak, erupted in the south-west. It sought an end to foreign interference and demanded reform of Korean castes. Japan and China both dispatched troops to quell it, sparking the Sino-Japanese War. Gojeong tried to play foreign powers off against one other, but was out of his depth and undermined by local factions and violent plotters favouring one power or the other. Japanese assassins murdered his pro-Russian queen; Gojeong fled to the Russian legation. Meanwhile, Japan, which was winning the Sino-Japanese War, pressured Gojeong, in the Gabo Reforms of 1894, to update his institutions, including abolishing castes and banning slavery. In 1897 Gojeong declared the 'Great Korean Empire', effectively ending the ancient vassal state relationship with China.

▲ An official portrait of King Gojeong, Joseon's last independent king. Though he attempted to modernize Korea, his small, weak kingdom became the prize in a regional power struggle.

Japan won the Sino-Japanese War in 1895, fought alongside Western powers in China's Boxer Rebellion in 1900, then defeated Russia in 1905. London and Washington, contemptuous of Beijing and wary of Moscow, welcomed Tokyo's ascendency in a peninsula lying well beyond their own spheres of interest. In 1905 Japan asserted control over Korea's external relations. Activists responded with assassinations, but there was no national resistance. In 1910 the powerless Gojeong saw his dynasty end as his kingdom was annexed. For 35 years Korea disappeared from global minds and global maps.

▶ Morning calm under rising sun

In its colony, Japan installed modern administration, law and education. Through investments in infrastructure and industry, a modern economy appeared. There were many benefits. Fine buildings arose; the largest industrial complex in the Japanese empire was built in north-east Korea; media, literature and film flourished; Japanese and local-owned companies were created and listed on a stock exchange; education expanded; the national life expectancy and population increased.

But Korea was a colony, and colonies are exploited. Koreans were subjects of Japan but lacked the rights of citizens. Buddhist temples were restored, but Koreans were pressured to worship at Shinto shrines. Research was conducted into historical sites, but local artworks were taken from Korea to the metropole; Joseon's palaces were dismantled and turned into public spaces. Agricultural yields improved, but much rice was exported to Japan. There was resentment, particularly as Korea had – unlike many colonies in Africa, the Middle East and South-east Asia – been a unified polity since the seventh century.

Exacerbating humiliation was the fact that Japan's takeover had been a walk-in, not an invasion. There was guerrilla resistance in the early years and a spectacularly idealistic and brutally repressed independence movement in 1919, but, latterly, the peninsula was quiescent. Post-1919, resistance grew beyond Korean borders. On the political right, a provisional government established itself in Shanghai; on the left, communist guerrillas would battle Japanese forces in Manchuria.

The Great Depression of 1929 had a heavy impact on Japan. Subsequently, the cultured, refined and modern island nation that had so impressed the West and fought alongside the allies in World War I was submerged beneath violent politics, paranoid nationalism and aggressive militarism. Korea was the springboard for Japan's march into Manchuria in 1931 and its invasion of China in 1937. The colony was ruthlessly mobilized as a supply base for the Japanese emperor's voracious armies as they punched deeper into China and policies assimilated Koreans more than heretofore. In 1939 Koreans were pressured to assume Japanese names; in the 1940s all official documents were written in Japanese and in 1943 Korean-language education was banned.

In 1941 Japan, allied with Hitler's Germany, went to war with the Western powers. Hundreds of thousands of Koreans served in Japanese uniform or as industrial labour. Some volunteered: there were Korean generals, anti-partisan units and kamikaze pilots; Korean prison-camp guards were feared by allied POWs for their brutality. Other Koreans were coerced, tricked or forced into service. Most notoriously, thousands, perhaps tens of thousands (records are unclear) of Korean girls were used as 'comfort women' – prostitutes servicing the imperial military – alongside Japanese, Chinese, South-east Asian and even a handful of European females.

After early Axis successes, the tide turned. Japan's army – a force that has been called the bravest and cruellest in history – fought with to-the-last-man resistance against Britain in Burma and the United States in the Pacific. But when Moscow declared war on Tokyo in World War II's final days and the Red Army stormed into Manchuria and northern Korea, the emperor's forces collapsed. On 15 August 1945 Japan surrendered after two atomic bombings. Tokyo's defeat spelled freedom for Korea and, while much of Europe and Asia was laid waste, the peninsula had suffered virtually no physical damage from the war. In the power vacuum, a left-leaning political grouping set up the Korean People's Republic (KPR), with 'People's Committees' nationwide.

This promising state of affairs would not last. The Allied powers had made decisions for Japan's colony without seeking the input of a single Korean, and after three decades of colonial rule, potential leaders of an independent Korea were polarized by background, experience and political outlook. Combined with a new bipolar global power structure, the scene was set for a new round of devastation just five years after history's greatest war had ended.

▶ Two Koreas, two Koreans

In 1943, in the Egyptian capital Cairo, China, the UK and the United States agreed that all Japan's colonies would be freed after the war; in 1945, at Yalta, the three, plus the USSR, agreed on four-power trusteeship with independence to follow. With the Soviet juggernaut rolling into northern Korea, Americans urgently realized that Moscow might swallow the entire peninsula before US troops could land. On 10 August 1945 two American officers were given 30 minutes to find a demarcation line: using a National Geographic map, they chose the 38th parallel. This line was communicated to the Soviets, who, rather to US surprise, halted at the parallel. Korea had been meat-cleavered in two.

The Soviets worked with the KPR in the north: land reforms were enacted, industry nationalized. On 8 September US troops walked ashore at Seoul's port, Incheon, to be greeted by crowds of Koreans, delighted at liberation from Japan. But the GIs were combat troops without experience in nation-building. Ignoring the KPR, the Americans appalled Koreans by operating via existing, colonial-era power structures.

Both Korea's new occupiers imported favourites as potential leaders. Moscow's man arrived in September. The 33-year-old Kim Il-sung had led a band of communist guerrillas against the Japanese in Manchuria in the 1930s and even (briefly) liberated the small Korean town of Pochonbo. After the Japanese stepped up their counter-insurgency (using Korean special units, among others), Kim retreated to the Russian Far East and became an officer in the Red Army, where he sat out World War II. In 1946 the charismatic and dynamic Kim set up a proto-government and the nucleus of an army.

Washington's man was the 65-year-old Rhee Syngman, an independence lobbyist and ex-president of the provisional government in Shanghai who arrived home in October 1945. Rhee spoke English, held degrees from Princeton and Harvard, and, fervently anti-communist, strongly denounced the KPR. In 1946 Rhee, like Kim, started laying the basis for government.

In December 1945 the four-power trusteeship plan was dropped, but attempts to find a unified political solution for Korea sputtered. Polarization increased. In 1947 Washington put the situation before the newly created United Nations (UN). Against Soviet protests, the UN mandated nationwide elections. The UN supervisory body was refused access to the North, so elections went ahead only in the South in May 1948. The Republic of Korea (ROK) was established (the name referenced both the Korean Empire and the Shanghai provisional government) with Rhee as president in Seoul. In August, Pyongyang held elections and Kim was made premier of the Democratic People's Republic of Korea (DPRK). The South held the bulk of the population and Korea's prime agricultural land; the North controlled most natural resources and the Japanese-era heavy industry.

Soviet troops withdrew in 1948, US troops in 1949; both left military advisors to build up their respective armies. Communist uprisings had flared in the South and had been repressed by US-advised South Korean troops: as many as 30,000 were killed in brutal operations on Jeju Island, off Korea's south coast. Border fighting also broke out along the 38th parallel, but with Rhee having made no secret of his desire to march north, Washington withheld offensive weapons, such as tanks and heavy artillery. With communist uprisings in the South suppressed and revolution presumably obviated, Kim, reinforced by contingents of battle-hardened Korean troops returning home after fighting with Mao Zedong's forces in the Chinese Civil War, began badgering a cautious Stalin to let him attack south. Eventually, Stalin agreed. Kim was supplied with tanks, artillery and aircraft, while Soviet advisors helped plan 'Operation Storm' – its object the reunification of Korea under the red banner.

▶ Apocalypse

In the early hours of 25 June 1950, thunder was heard from the frontier. It was artillery – not an unusual sound during border clashes. But the barrage was followed by brigades of tanks and divisions of infantry. This was no tactical raid; this was a strategic invasion: the Korean War had begun. Despite brave resistance in some areas – using Japanese tactics, some ROK troops tied explosives to themselves and dived under advancing armour – Kim's Korean People's Army (KPA) seized Seoul three days into the war.

With South Korea collapsing, Americans, seeing a global communist plot, seeded a counter-plot. The Soviet Union was boycotting the UN as a protest against Taiwan holding the Chinese seat, so Washington enlisted the world body in defence of Rhee's government. The United States forces, led by General Douglas MacArthur, would lead the UN Command (UNC); US and ROK troops would eventually be joined by 15 combatant nations.

American units, fresh from relaxed occupation in Japan, proved easy meat for the KPA in early battles, but, amid desperate fighting, US reinforcements and the remains of the ROK Army established a fragile battle line in the south-east – the 'Pusan Perimeter' – which surrounded all that remained of South Korea. MacArthur, a master of amphibious warfare, had a card to play that the KPA, whose air force had been destroyed and whose navy was insignificant, had no response to. Embarking marines on a landing fleet, he landed at Incheon. The KPA, breaking its teeth on the Pusan Perimeter, now had an enemy 200 miles to its rear. Disengaging, the KPA faded into the hills and struggled northward. Seoul was retaken in September.

▲ South Korean soldiers pass through a devastated village, after crossing the 38th parallel.

With South Korea liberated, the UNC attacked over the 38th parallel to finish Kim and unify Korea. Mechanized columns raced for the Yalu River, the border with China; objectives tumbled like dominoes. With the KPA disintegrating, Stalin advised Kim to retreat into China and prepare a guerrilla campaign. As autumn darkened to winter, relieved UNC troops were told they would be 'home by Christmas'. In fact, they were advancing into the twentieth century's greatest ambush.

Mao had been watching the drama with concern. Korea marked China's strategic north-east flank; twice before, in the 1590s and 1930s, Japan had used Korea as an invasion route. Moreover, Manchuria was a seat of industry, and Mao feared MacArthur would not halt at the Yalu. Stalin was deeply moved to learn that Mao was infiltrating troops – called the 'Chinese People's Volunteer Army' (CPVA) to maintain the appearance of neutrality – into Korea's freezing mountains. Lightly equipped Chinese would be facing massive firepower – Mao's son Anying was killed by a UNC airstrike in the first days of combat – and they had few illusions about the hazards ahead: they dubbed the Yalu River crossings 'The Gates of Hell'. But they were tough, experienced fighters and they had some surprising tactics.

For UNC troops, everything changed with terrifying swiftness. Veterans recall distant hills changing colour as the Chinese swarmed down; of signal bugles blowing in darkness; of murderous chaos. The Chinese tactic was the 'Human Wave'. Camouflaged Chinese would mass before a UNC position, then charge at close range. Meanwhile, other Chinese would flow around flanks – like water – and establish ambushes on the UNC line of communications. The road-bound UNC was routed. A ROK corps disintegrated; two regiments of US infantry were shattered in a death ride through the Kunu-ri Pass, and, at Chosin Reservoir, crack US marines narrowly escaped annihilation by fighting through a harrowing mountain trap. In Washington, President Harry Truman raised the possibility of atomic retaliation.

To deny infrastructure to the enemy, retreating UNC troops left behind 'scorched earth'. In sub-zero winter conditions, some 600,000 to 700,000 Korean refugees, mainly old people, women and children, joined the hellish exodus. Seoul fell again on 4 January, but now the CPVA was at the end of its supply lines. The UNC, deploying firepower against manpower, mastered subsequent Chinese offensives. In April the largest offensive of the war was unleashed when a third of a million communists attacked, aiming to annihilate the UNC and seize Seoul. It failed – though a British battalion was destroyed in an epic stand on the Imjin River.

It was the last big manoeuvre. By summer 1951 the war was stalemated along the 38th parallel. Peace negotiations began, but Stalin told Kim and Mao to keep fighting, to bleed the United States dry; the communist side also falsified biological warfare claims. The US Air Force pummelled North Korea relentlessly while duelling MIGs (many piloted by Russians and Chinese) above the Yalu. Below, troops dug in, and the conflict became a series of bloody fights for the next hill. Soldier-poet Yi Tok-chin wrote: 'The landscape changes as corpses pile up / And this ridge becomes a bloodthirsty devil.' Peace talks dragged on.

For UNC troops, war in a barren, brutalized land was hideous. Both sides committed atrocities. Harsh weather made soldiering painful; rugged terrain made casualty evacuation tortuous. The Chinese attacked en masse, up close, in darkness – a particularly terrifying form of combat. Destruction was biblical, with the extensive UNC firepower – particularly napalm, a sticky, incendiary gel which burns at temperatures eight times hotter than boiling water – generating colossal damage. Some soldiers had a racist hatred of Koreans; others assisted orphans and civilians with charitable acts. To this day, Chaplain Russell Blaisdell ('The Father of a Thousand'), who airlifted orphans to safety, and Captain Leonard La Rue, whose ship evacuated 14,000 desperate Koreans from the North, are revered in South Korea.

Koreans underwent new experiences. Never before had so many different foreigners tramped Korean soil. Neither had so many modern goods – from rations to medicines, from jeeps to bibles, the bounty of Uncle Sam and charitable/religious groups – been so available. Corruption soared among administrators, feral 'slicky boys' connived and stole, and desperate women prostituted themselves in sordid shacks. But important skills were mastered. Thousands of Koreans studied English. The US Army trained Korean officers, teaching goal-setting, leadership, planning and organization – the basics of management. Engineers learned to fix machinery and build infrastructure.

ALL THAT MATTERS: MODERN KOREA

Entrepreneurs working for UNC forces learned pitching, accounting and invoicing. Refugees without prior experience of mercantilism embarked upon survival capitalism in scratch markets that rose in towns, villages and base perimeters.

At midnight, 27 July 1953, it stopped. An armistice had been signed in a border truce village, Panmunjeom. Rhee, whose goal was unification, was infuriated and released communist POWs (who defected) in a move that endangered the armistice. Washington and (later) Beijing signed defence treaties with their allies, and US troops would remain in the South. The two Koreas would be separated by a 4-kilometre-wide (2.5-mile) 'Demilitarized Zone' (DMZ). The war consumed as many as 2 million lives. China lost 183,108, the United States 33,741 and the United Kingdom 1,109, but most of the dead were Korean.

▶ Legacy and aftermath

Korea was the UN's first war, the Cold War's first 'hot war' and the United States' first 'limited war'. It was the only war in which the superpowers clashed, and marked the only (counter-) invasion by Free World forces of a communist state. Yet Korea never achieved the profile of World War II: the war's outbreak was more complicated, its morals cloudier, the enemy leaders not as demonizable as Hitler, the conclusion inconclusive. Moreover, Korea would soon be overshadowed by the United States' next war in Asia, captured in all its glamour and horror on colour TV; Korea survives only on black-and-white newsreel. The national angst accompanying the United States' Vietnam adventure spawned fine filmic and literary treatments. Not so Korea; the astonishing drama of armies surging up and down the peninsula, with fortunes ever-changing – drama never equalled in the Vietnam fighting – is overlooked in popular culture. The conflict's static phase is recalled as old-fashioned drudgery. When Korea is remembered, it is dubbed 'The Forgotten War'.

The winners were the nations on Korea's periphery. Japan was enriched, its economy massively boosted by the neighbouring carnage. Today's China is considered an economic superpower, but by defeating the United States in North Korea and fighting it to a standstill in the South, China first gained status as a military superpower, a remarkable achievement for a peasant nation.

The losers were the Koreans. The holocaust solved nothing; the war ended, with slight adjustments, on its start line, leaving some 10 million people separated from family members. National division had been deepened, and distrust, bitterness and enmity exacerbated. Across the DMZ (today, the world's most heavily militarized frontier), brother faced brother. No peace treaty has been signed; the war continues.

Most UN troops were only too happy to depart the barren hills, stinking paddies, pathetic orphans and countless graves. But Korea's impact is deep: some, haunted by those midnight battles, sleep with the lights on six decades later. Given the devastation of South Korea, the poverty of its inhabitants and the venality of its administrators, few dared hope that the nation they defended would somehow forge a shining future.

While an examination of Korea's social culture and historical trends would require a book of its own, it is important to understand some of these roots, for they are the threads linking ancient times to modern.

In Korea, authority is delivered through vertical hierarchies: to communicate, Koreans need to establish who is senior in order to use the appropriate grammatical format. In this top-down structure, national power changed hands through overthrows, coups and intrigues rather than rebellions or revolutions from below. Yet society is deeply communal, because Koreans traditionally subsisted on rice-farming, a form of agriculture demanding close co-operation among villagers. Hence, group identity is prized over individualism; a strong sense of egalitarianism, even entitlement, persists.

Feudal classes were demolished in the late nineteenth century, so today's society is a series of concentric rings: family; hometown and province; school and university; army unit and company; ultimately, nation. Most twenty-first-century Koreans are just one or two generations removed from ancestral hometowns, hence the extraordinary traffic jams as urbanized families depart for grandparents' villages during national holidays. Regional identities remain strong, and vanished kingdoms persist in geopolitics: North Korea represents Goguryeo; Silla (south-east) and Baekje (south-west) represent regional voting blocks in South Korean elections. Koreans are also part of extended clans based on surname and geographical origins (there is a very limited number of surnames; half of all Koreans are named Kim, Park or Lee). These various relationship webs grant all Koreans supportive social networks, and, with their communal instincts, they slot effectively into groups and teams. But relationships include obligations, engendering favouritism, nepotism and corruption.

Many Koreans are superstitious. The ancient native religion is shamanism; remarkably, it survives both independently – shamans tell fortunes and carry out good-luck rituals, with conglomerate chairmen reportedly among their clients – and as an influence upon the imported religions, Buddhism and Christianity. Confucianism provided Joseon's core philosophy, hence Korea was male-centric and reverential towards ancestors. Education, providing a meritocratic vehicle for any male to raise his social standing via bureaucratic exams, was prized; this reverence survives into the modern age.

But, among the educated, there has always been factional struggle between forces favouring orthodoxy and those promoting heterodoxy. For example: educated Koreans produced the world's first moveable metal type (1234) and a brilliantly simply phonetic alphabet, hangeul (1443–4), that can be learned in hours. This medieval IT was suppressed by conservatism. Metal type was later reinvented (and disseminated) elsewhere, while hangeul was stifled by aristocratic literati who prized Chinese characters (it was not disseminated via national education until Japanese rule). Had these two technologies been integrated and disseminated earlier, Korea might have become a very different nation.

Korea has always been overshadowed by stronger foreign powers, its inhabitants tugged between co-operation and resistance. Much factionalism in modern Korea stems from attitudes towards foreign forces and influences. For or against? And if for – which power to ally with, which influence to adopt? The Korean Peninsula was first united by Silla, which crushed Goguryeo in alliance with China's Tang Dynasty and then turned on Tang. Today's Koreans are taught that their nation is unique in the number of foreign invasions it has suffered, but most of Joseon's six hundred years were peaceful, bar a savage Japanese assault in the sixteenth century and two Manchurian invasions in the seventeenth. The twentieth century would be Korea's most traumatic, and, as victims of colonialism, division and war, Koreans adopted a fierce nationalism. Post-war, the competing states adopted extreme approaches to the outside world: one would be enriched by engagement, the other impoverished by isolation.

What of inner life? Unlike their 'inscrutable' island neighbours, Koreans are richly emotional. *Shinpparam* means 'wind of exuberance'; and communal joy was expressed in the singing and dancing of village festivals, misery in wailing at funerals or other misfortunes. Emoting is constant – at sports events, in popular culture and even in demonstrations and debates (both online and parliamentary). *Nunchi* – unspoken sensitivity to others' emotions – is important, so that status, or 'face', is maintained. Two feelings are considered particularly Korean: *han* is a sense of repressed bitterness over unresolved wrongs; *jeong* a sense of bonding and empathy.

All these socio-cultural constants have a bearing on the two Koreas' political and economic trajectories.

2

Economic miracle

*'Even from a small stream,
a dragon can arise.'*

Korean proverb

▶ General manager...

Seoul, 16 May 1961. Passers-by looked on in consternation: military vehicles blocked intersections and bridges; government offices and broadcasting stations swarmed with armed troops. Dominating this activity, surrounded by heavily armed paratroopers, paced a hard-faced general in windcheater and sunglasses. Visionary but pragmatic; pro-Japanese but nationalistic; a killer but a nation-builder – this man had big plans. Few figures in Korean history would bequeath a stronger legacy to their land. His name was Park Chung-hee.

Born to peasants in 1917, Park been attended by fortune even before his birth: his mother had attempted abortion – unsuccessfully. He stood just five foot four but crackled with restless energy. Briefly a schoolmaster, he had volunteered for the Japanese Army, graduated from the Manchukuo Military Academy and the elite Tokyo Military Academy, then, like many colonial officers, joined the ROK Army. Like other thoughtful Koreans, Park dallied with the Left: in a shadowy episode in 1948, he was imprisoned for heading an army communist cell. His luck held: superiors interceded with President Rhee and his execution was cancelled. (Some sources claim that he was saved by betraying his co-conspirators.) During the war he rose to the rank of brigadier, then underwent training in artillery and logistics at America's Fort Sill. By 1961 he was the ROK Army's chief-of-staff for operations.

By the time Park stalked on to the scene, Rhee, disgraced, was exiled. The president had executed his democratic opponents and suppressed the media. The economy drifted; corruption was rampant. In 1960 Rhee won a rigged election. Citizens protested. The police responded, and a schoolboy was killed by a tear-gas grenade through his skull. Riots broke out in Seoul: police opened a murderous fire. It was the final straw. Rhee resigned and was whisked away by the CIA to Hawaii, where he died in 1965.

A democratic government, sharing power between President Yun Bo-seon and Prime Minister Chang Myong, took office. It proved unworkable. Factionalism undermined governance; order broke down. Watching from the wings was the army. Park plotted. When he heard that students planned to march to the DMZ, Park rallied troops (including MPs ordered to arrest him) with a speech calling for military revolution to restore order and smash corruption. The coup was on.

It proved effective and (almost) bloodless. Neither Chang nor Yoon came out strongly against the decisive general. First, Park seized full control of the coup leadership, then created a powerful machine of observation and repression, the Korean CIA (KCIA). In 1963 – be-suited, not uniformed, as US President John Kennedy demanded civilian rule – Park was elected president.

Among his first moves was an offensive against corruption. Heavily implicated was the merchant class. Cowed businessmen, marched through streets in dunce caps, holding signs reading 'I am a corrupt pig', immediately realized who the new boss was. Banks were nationalized. Park had seized South Korea's economic helm. Now he could implement an audacious vision.

In 1960 South Korea's economy was on a par with Ghana's. It had no natural resources, competitive advantage or experience of global trade. Park planned to reconstruct the country from the ground up with capitalism – but not the laissez-faire American variety. Private enterprise would form the engine; the state would steer. This hierarchical concept placed a very Korean body – an elite bureaucracy, the Economic Planning Board – as control tower over the commercial class. Favoured firms would be assigned projects, sectors and scarce capital. Their products would be incubated in a protected environment that banned imports of finished goods. Consumption would be dampened, production emphasized. Park made a virtue – competitiveness – out of necessity – hard currency shortfalls: he told his companies to export. Without this element, Park's model would have given birth to modern companies, but not necessarily good ones. By battling it out in global markets, Korean firms were forced to become competitive. At home, Park incentivized management with export targets; success was rewarded with further projects. Exports were 'good'; imports 'bad'. Of course, Korea had to import raw materials, but would re-export them, with value added. Meanwhile, the US alliance would be leveraged to maintain 'most favoured nation' trade status in the world's largest market.

All Park's experiences were marshalled. Educated technocrats wrote economic blueprints; military-style managers executed them. State-led development, with co-operation between government and military, was based on his experience of the military-industrial complex in Manchukuo; many key appointees would be ex-officers. 'Five-year plans' bore the hallmarks of communism, while goal-oriented management reflected Fort Sill training. But Park had a problem: Koreans' traditional distaste for business and manpower. 'In the early Western accounts of Korea, you never see a reference to diligence,' said Robert Neff, the leading historian of early foreigners in Korea. 'It's all lazy, lazy, lazy.' If Park were to re-engineer his economy, he first had to re-engineer his human resources.

▶ ...economic warriors

Koreans have always held a Confucian respect for education: during the war, professors had raised tents behind the front, teaching knowledge-hungry off-duty soldiers. Expanding upon the mass education of the colonial era, Seoul invested heavily (as much as 19 per cent of budget). Universal primary education arrived in the 1960s, secondary education in the 1980s. Conformity, numeracy and literacy (the latter made possible by Korea's phonetic alphabet, hangeul) were emphasized. Discipline, obedience and teamwork were further inculcated during military service.

Via schooling, the military, slogans and mass movements, a 'can do' spirit was instilled. Students, labourers and office workers ('salarymen') started their days performing group 'citizen calisthenics'. Songs with titles like 'Let's Get Rich!' were promoted, posters blared 'Let's live well together!' and morning affirmations such as 'We were born with the mission of modernizing our nation!' were chanted in colleges, offices and factories. Korean peasants had endured seasonal hard labour and survival capitalism during the war: now, industrial diligence was promoted as the core virtue. Koreans were harangued to study hard, work hard, live hard. Everything was to be done 'Palli, palli!' ('Quickly, quickly!') – a phrase that became a syndrome. A 'hungry *jongshin* [feeling]' – a hunger for success – was cultivated.

Companies were managed like regiments. Chairmen's words were law, enabling speedy management; neither shareholders nor unions had a say. New employees underwent boot-camp-style induction programmes to instil drive and loyalty; the media carried photos of determined-looking Korean workers in military-style formations. Leisure was for wimps: Koreans worked six-day weeks with just a week's annual holiday. In their (rare) moments off, they played hard. Cigarettes and *soju* (a vodka-like grain spirit) enjoyed low tax regimes. While executives cut deals in shady 'room saloons' staffed by attractive females, workers and managers bonded, strengthening their *jeong* over barbequed pork in heroic drinking sessions. Family life was a casualty of work life, but paternalistic managers attended workers' family events, such as weddings and funerals.

With South Korea riddled with factionalism and regionalism, nationalism was promoted as both unifying force and spur against external competition. Government urged the people to overcome the dreaded North Korea and – invoking *han* – to overtake hated Japan. Suspicion of foreigners was inculcated in schoolchildren, who chanted: 'Don't trust America / Don't be cheated by Russia / Be cautious about China / Or Japan will rise again.' Park was derisive of Korea's underdevelopment and weakness but admired Japan, the first Asian nation to modernize and a benchmark for the branding of native assets. Japan had Kyoto? Very well, Korea had the Silla capital of Gyeongju. Japan had Mount Fuji? Korea had the scenic Mount Seorak. Japan had sumo; Korea had *ssireum*, a folk wrestling system. Japan had samurai; Korea had the Hwarang, a Silla youth corps And so on. The end result was a prickly, table-thumping national pride. Was the Korean alphabet not the most scientific in existence? Was local cuisine not the healthiest and tastiest? Was the native dog, the Jindo, not the most faithful, bravest hound on earth?

Above all, Koreans were motivated. With no class system, Park-era Korea was egalitarian, and education and hard work provided paths to enrichment and status. There was no longer an aristocratic or colonial overlord taking the fruits of labour but nor was there an alternative: in the absence of welfare, no work equalled no money. Many nineteenth- and early twentieth-century Western travellers had found Koreans indolent and backward; during the war, many foreign soldiers felt either sympathy or disdain. Visiting foreign businessmen in the 1960s and 1970s discovered a formidable new breed – proud, hard-working, competitive. Some Europeans and Americans were dismissive of early Korean industrial efforts. Soon they would know better. Lacking natural resources – Korea's gold, hydroelectric power and minerals, not to mention its colonial-era industrial base, all lay in the North – these economic warriors were the only attribute South Korea possessed. Park would leverage them to the hilt.

▶ Planning and capitalization

South Korea's development strategy in the 1950s had been import subsidization – that is, making things at home rather than importing them. Early industrialization focused on 'The Three Whites': textiles, sugar and flour (flour was easier to produce than rice). The key businessman in these sectors had started his company under colonial rule. This was Lee Byung-chull; his company was called 'Three Stars' – or 'Samsung' in Korean. Other firms prominent in import subsidization were Hanwha, which created local dynamite in 1958, and Goldstar (later Lucky Goldstar; today LG), which built Korea's first radio in 1959.

Park was more ambitious: he wanted not import substitution but exports, and exports more valuable than wigs and textiles; and not just light industry – Samsung's specialization – but heavy industry. This demanded basics like cement and steel. While Japan was one model, Park's most important influence was West Germany.

In 1964 Park visited a country that was divided, like his own, but which was on a fast-track recovery from 1945. German autobahns impressed Park greatly; he determined to benchmark them. From there, went the logic, build cars to run on them. Moreover, autos require steel, components and refined oil. In other words: build roads, then industrialize around them. This became Park's blueprint.

To fund it, Park needed hard currency, but US aid had peaked in 1958: from then on, dollars declined. So, among South Korea's early exports was its only resource – people. Park dispatched three divisions of troops to fight alongside the United States in Vietnam. The Korean troops proved effective, tough and brutal: 'The Prussians of Asia', as one US officer noted. Critically, they were paid in dollars. Meanwhile, Korean businessmen flooded into Vietnam on contracts. Japan had enjoyed collateral bounty from the Korean War; Korea would enjoy similar from Vietnam. US payments to South Korea during the war amounted to US$1 billion; the cost was 5,099 dead soldiers. Meanwhile, Park dispatched nurses and miners to West Germany following his visit: they remitted home US$100 million.

Park also turned to Japan. In 1965 Tokyo coughed up US$800 million: US$200 million in soft loans, US$300 million in commercial loans and US$300 million in compensation for colonialism. In return, Tokyo and Seoul opened diplomatic relations. Furious Koreans protested; Park forged ahead. He distributed none of Tokyo's cash to colonial victims such as forced labourers or comfort women, for he had bigger plans: to build a Seoul–Busan highway and POSCO, a steel plant. US officials and the World Bank advised against such projects; Park characteristically ignored them.

▶ Rise of the Titans

The highway opened in 1970, the steel mill in 1973. POSCO's head was a classic Park appointee. Park Tae-joon, 'The Man with Iron Blood', was an ex-military officer who leveraged colonial-era Japanese university connections to obtain Japanese technical assistance. He lived and slept alongside his workers, overseeing POSCO's construction from a bunker called 'The Rommel House' after the famed general. But POSCO, a national company, was unusual. Park preferred private businessmen, running around 50 key companies. Dominant among them, and a key figure in the highway project, was a Park favourite. Chung Ju-yung was a feisty North Korean refugee who bonded with his workers by wrestling. He had started business in delivery and accountancy during the colonial era, then did contracts for the US military. When the highway opened, Park is said to have told Chung that, now Korea had the road, it needed cars. Chung took him at his word: his company was named 'Modern' – in Korean, 'Hyundai'.

With the highway, the backbone of a modern road network, and hot steel coming online, Park opened his second phase. Six industries – steel, autos, shipbuilding, electronics, machinery and petrochemicals – were emphasized. Foreign partners assisted early efforts with technology, consulting and investment – British in ships, Americans and Japanese in cars, Japanese in steel. Hyundai entered construction, ships and autos:

▲ The Hyundai shipyards in Ulsan are the largest in the world, stretching 4 kilometres (2.5 miles) along the coast of Mipo Bay.

legendarily, Chung convinced his first ship buyer of Korean skills in the industry by showing him a banknote with a 'turtle ship' – an ironclad warship of the 1590s – on it. In reality, he had no experience; the ship and shipyard (today, the world's largest) were built simultaneously. Meanwhile, Samsung entered electronics and shipbuilding. Another firm, led by dynamic entrepreneur Kim Woo-joong, went into electronics, autos and ships. Kim's firm was 'Great Universe', or 'Daewoo'.

Early Korean exports were priced low; market share was prioritized over profitability, a strategy subsidized by high domestic prices. (Even today, many Korean products cost more at home than abroad.) Whether

Koreans liked it or not was immaterial: South Korea was a producer-, not a consumer-, economy. Koreans were urged to save; resultant capital was channelled to industry. Specialized finance firms like Industrial Bank of Korea, Korea Exchange Bank and Korea Development Bank appeared to fund exporters.

Management was untrammelled by bothersome regulation: corners were cut, labour laws unapplied. From the 1960s to the Millennium, Korean products were copycats (earning Korea a dismal reputation for intellectual property violations). Naturally, they lacked polish; writer Mike Breen noted that Koreans' 'can do' attitude merged with 'that'll do' execution. In the 1980s US comedians got endless mileage from Hyundai car jokes. (Sample: 'How do you make a Hyundai go over 60?' 'Push it over a cliff.') Lee Keun-hee, Lee Byung-chull's son who succeeded him as Samsung chairman, was appalled to discover Samsung devices on the bottom shelves of US retailers. Back home, he smashed a pile of them, urging executives to 'Change everything but your wife and kids!' Other errors were fatal. In a pair of deadly accidents in the mid-1990s, a bridge and a department store collapsed in Seoul, and Korean Air suffered a string of crashes from the 1970s to the 1990s.

But Koreans learned fast. As global trade expanded and new markets opened, they climbed the value ladder. Daewoo's Kim, who titled his autobiography *Every Street is Paved with Gold*, exulted, 'The world is wide, and work is plentiful!' The model continued to deliver. Park was assassinated in 1979, but under his successor growth surged. In 1970 South Korea's GDP had been US$8 billion; in 1975 it was US$21.1 billion; in 1980, US$ 62.2 billion; and, in 1985, US$93.4 billion.

This was not just due to strategic investments. The 1980s marked Japan's ascent to economic superstardom, and in 1985 Tokyo appreciated the yen. Japan was South Korea's main rival in most sectors; a strengthened yen made Japanese products more expensive than Korean. In 1986 South Korea recorded its first-ever trade surplus. In 1987 it was US$10 billion; in 1988 it was US$15 billion. That year, South Korea hosted the Summer Olympics – in no small part due to extravagant lobbying by Hyundai's Chung. In the build-up, there was massive infrastructure spend: the Han River was dredged, subways were expanded, and a national phone network (with switching technologies developed by government research institutes) was put in place.

South Korea's coming-out party fortuitously showcased the nation as a business partner to Eastern European nations emerging from communism. A slogan, 'The Miracle on the Han' – named for Seoul's river – was promoted. (Korean branders, like Korean companies, were unoriginal thinkers: the phrase borrowed Germany's 'Miracle on the Rhine'.) It was appropriate. Korea had gone from agrarian basket case in the 1950s to industrial powerhouse in the 1980s and was being talked of as another Japan. In 1985 *Newsweek* declared, 'Here Comes Korea, Inc.'

The country had changed physically. Inspired by German reforestation, Park copied it in Korea. Many landscapes had been deforested by centuries of wood-fuelled heating and colonial logging: now, they were re-carpeted in green. Park implemented the 'Saemaul Undong' ('New Village Movement') to modernize the backward countryside. In rural areas, concrete and corrugated iron replaced wood and thatch. Subsequently, in urban areas in the 1980s and 1990s, gigantic, identical apartment complexes rose as the population shifted: 50 per cent of South Koreans lived in the countryside in 1970; by 1990, 81.9 per cent of them lived in urban areas. Similar projects in Western countries became slums, but, for communal Koreans, 'aparts' became aspirational. However, these ruthlessly utilitarian, efficiency-centric transformations raped Korea's aesthetics. All urban areas started looking the same; once-delightful rural vistas were made hideous with concrete.

▶ Trouble ahead

Targeted investment in the 1960s and 1970s had transformed South Korea from chump to champ. But in the late 1980s and 1990s investment became over-exuberant. By the 1980s the national champions Park had incubated were giant, diversified groups: family-run conglomerates, or *chaebol.* With Park's white-knuckled grip on the economy gone, 'me too' investments were increasingly overlapping and unprofitable and diluted core competencies. The term 'chips to ships' fitted Samsung, Hyundai and Daewoo; this was 'survival of the fattest'.

Meanwhile, *chaebol* were suffering unaccustomed problems. Labour, suppressed for decades, blossomed after democratization in 1987. Protests and strikes were bitter. Moreover, *chaebol* were family managed and chairmanships started to pass from the safe hands of first-generation bosses into those of the second. Some, such as Samsung's Lee, who had spearheaded the conglomerate's move into semiconductors, were competent, but it was unclear whether all successors were fit for the task. Compounding the problems was infighting: while politics was riven by factionalism, conglomerates suffered sibling rivalries.

Under Park, links between government and business had always been tight, but Park was clean: he never enriched himself or his family. Not so his successors in the presidential Blue House. Corruption tied business to politics, with state-controlled finance in the middle. These relationships were not just morally dubious: they were economically damaging, stripping rationality and prudence from decision-making, capital allocation and risk calibration.

By the mid-1990s the environment was risk-heavy. In 1995 South Korea appreciated the won to tame inflation, then Japan was struck by the Kobe earthquake and the yen plunged. Korean exports were hit: in 1996 the country suffered a record trade deficit of US$23 billion. Moreover, Korean banks had had their overseas lending ceilings raised by government in 1993. Lacking expertise, they invested US$25 billion in booming South-east Asia. Thus the country's international exposures were US$48 billion, but Seoul's foreign exchange reserves were just US$20 billion. These were bad numbers for a country that had, in 1996, joined the OECD and was the world's eleventh largest economy.

The year 1997 dawned with bad news: Hanbo Iron and Steel collapsed in January under massive debts – only the first in a line of over-extended, second-tier *chaebol* to tumble. In February, Sammi Steel went under. Nervous creditors started recalling Korean loans. In April, Daenong Group imploded; in May, Jinro. Korean firms' debt–equity ratios (i.e. ratios of borrowing to assets) were, on average, 400 per cent, but Jinro – the premier producer of the national spirit *soju*, ergo a business akin to printing money – had piled up debts of *40 times* equity. In June, the automotive manufacturer Kia followed. In July, South-east Asia's property bubble burst. Thailand, Indonesia and Malaysia were engulfed in an economic storm. Korean bankruptcies continued. In September, New Core Group fell; in November, Haitai Group went under. That month, Bloomberg ran a downbeat story on Korea's economy; its Seoul office received a bomb threat. Korean bureaucrats berated naysayers in the foreign media and financial communities, trying to downplay the crisis. Their head-in-the-sand reaction convinced few. In December, Halla Group imploded. The stock market and currency were in free fall; foreign reserves evaporated. An economic tsunami loomed over Korea, Inc. Would the 'economic miracle' be crushed?

Man on fire: Korea's labour movement

On 13 November 1970 a young man stood outside the 'Peace Market' in Cheonggeycheon, central Seoul – a notorious sweatshop district where young female textile workers worked 16-hour days for pitiful wages in Dickensian conditions. He emptied gasoline over himself, lit a match and flared up. 'Workers are not machines!' he screamed. 'Let us rest on Sundays!' Then he collapsed. His agonizing wounds were untreatable; he died within hours.

Chon Tae-il's sacrifice started a national debate, and he become a hero of Korea's labour movement. For three decades, Korean workers' rights were overlooked. Working conditions broke labour laws; union leaders were government stooges; bosses could employ state goons, and they even deployed male workers against female strikers.

Yet Seoul did upgrade labour. The first vocational schools – mechanical, electronics and construction – had appeared in 1968. Those with skills useful to industry were exempted from military service. And, as Korean industry climbed the value chain, bonuses began to reflect output: many workers, anxious to expand discretionary income, voluntarily agreed to long hours.

Even so, after democratization in 1987, the dam of discontent burst. Industrial actions soared: over 3,000 labour-management conflicts took place in the first three months, exceeding the total of the previous two decades. Student demonstrations had been common fodder for international news in the 1980s. In the 1990s this was replaced by footage of labour conflict, with militant unionists in headbands battling swarming riot police – who, during one huge strike in Ulsan ('Hyundai Town'), deployed landing craft and helicopters. Now labour had the upper hand, negotiating better wages, conditions and job security.

Among a workforce who sacrificed themselves for development and who believed in the dignity of labour, layoffs had been virtually impossible, but in 1998, amid crisis, there was no choice: labour flexibility increased. Still, even today, it is (in practice) extremely difficult for managers to trim workforces – hence massive increases in part-time and contract-based workers. Among these are hundreds of thousands of imported workers, largely from Central, South and South-east Asia, who do the 'DDD' ('dirty, difficult and dangerous') jobs young Koreans decline.

Today, labour militancy has dampened. Hyundai Motor's union ('The Aristocrats of Labour') remains powerful, and their strong bargaining stance and high wages partly explain Hyundai's enthusiastic offshoring. But Hyundai is untypical. While powerful, active unions remain in some sectors – autos, petrochemicals, finance, public service – they do not represent the overall economy, where the unionization rate is under 12 per cent and Korea's national flagship, Samsung, has no union. South Korean industry has overcome decades of bitterness, which speaks volumes about managerial flexibility and the loyalty of workers – who frown upon job-hopping – towards their companies.

Labour made the greatest sacrifices for South Korea's industrialization. Was it worth it? Tourists visiting Cheonggyecheon today will see a statue of Chon, but no 'Peace Market' – that has long gone. The area is now an attractive urban stream overlooked by restaurants, bars and coffee shops where working conditions are a world away from those Chon protested against with his life. He was just 22 years old.

▶ Fall and rise

Early crisis management was knee-jerk: media called for an old standby, anti-consumption campaigns. While these encouraged vandalization of foreign cars, the campaigns further hammered a reeling economy. In poignant scenes, citizens donated their gold at banks to pay off foreign debt; US$1.3 billion was raised. But this was just a drop in the ocean, and the glut impacted global gold prices. In December 1997, Korea elected long-time opposition leader Kim Dae-jung to the presidency. Kim proved equal to the task ahead, announcing that Korea could go bankrupt at any moment. After the previous prevarication, this was refreshing candour.

The International Monetary Fund (IMF) granted a US$58 billion bailout – then a record. In return, it demanded painful reforms. Koreans dubbed it 'The IMF Crisis'. High interest rates were set to stem capital outflow. Since the mid-1980s trade partners, notably the United States, had demanded South Korea open her domestic markets. Now, the IMF ordered Seoul to open its capital and real-estate markets. It told the government to sell bad banks and liberalize labour regulation. Previously, it had been almost impossible to fire people; the social compact was 'jobs for life'. Suddenly, there were 1.8 million unemployed. Bewildered workers toted signs reading, 'IMF: I'M Fired.' Speculation arose that Korea was the victim of an international financial conspiracy, and some media and industrialists denied the crisis: the problem was a financial shortfall; the important thing was that factories were running, they maintained. The contention that money is irrelevant to business is odd, but in Korea hardware had always been prioritized over software, scale over profit.

Chaebol slimmed down. Between 1998 and 2000 affiliates dropped 30 per cent. Under government-sponsored 'big deals', overlapping businesses were merged; Hyundai and LG's chip-making arms became Hynix. Companies entered state-enforced 'workouts' to bring debt down. In 1999 Daewoo Group collapsed under debts of US$80 billion: the world's then-biggest bankruptcy. Korea Inc.'s dodgy accountancy was starkly displayed: Daewoo had hidden debts of US$15 billion. Kim Woo-choong, an outspoken opponent of restructuring, fled abroad. Seoul nationalized some Daewoo arms, such as shipbuilding; others were sold. Following Hyundai founder Chung's death in 2001, his sons squabbled and the group split. The most prominent firms became Hyundai Motor (which acquired bankrupt Kia) and Hyundai Heavy, the shipbuilding arm. Samsung survived intact, though it sold its automotive arm – a subsidiary allegedly created by its chairman, a car fanatic.

Kim Dae-jung worked to overturn entrenched attitudes. He told Koreans to spend, reversing the old anti-consumption mantra. Historically, foreign investors had been unwelcome unless involved in technology transfer or joint ventures. Now Kim welcomed them. Samsung's car arm was bought by Renault; Daewoo's by GM; and investment funds acquired sinking banks. Foreign direct investment between 1998 and 2000 totalled US$40 billion, more than the accumulated total from 1962 to 1997.

Most critically, the Korean currency, the won, plummeted from KRW790 to the dollar to KRW1900. Cheap exports surged, delivering a foreign currency windfall. At the end of 1997, Korea had just US$4 billion in reserves; by 2002, US$116 billion had been accumulated. In June 1998, the stock market had been 280 points; by the end of 1999, it was at 1028. After a

6-per-cent economic contraction in 1998, Korea saw 10-per-cent growth in 1999 as the nation underwent a V-shaped recovery rather than the expected U-shaped upturn. Graduating from crisis ahead of time, Korea had astonished the world – again.

▶ Low savings, high technologies and global brands

Another crisis loomed in 2002. Hoping to end the country's export dependency, Seoul promoted consumption and easy credit. Educational spending rose, as did property prices – and mortgage costs. Previously unobtainable credit cards were handed out on streets; banks did minimal credit analysis. In 2003 South Korea was racked by a credit crisis. It was worked through, but by its end Koreans went from being some of the world's heaviest savers to carrying some of the world's heaviest household debt. To this day, local consumption is suppressed.

The global financial crisis of 2008 sent South Korea's stocks and currency reeling, but fundamentals were sound; the financial sector was not invested in US sub-prime. The country rebounded without the trauma of 1997–8. It had cushioned itself against export downturns by diversifying its trade portfolio beyond the United States and the European Union (EU). China is today South Korea's biggest export buyer and South Korea is China's biggest direct investor. Seoul also signed free trade agreements with the US and EU, ensuring Korean price advantages against Japanese and Chinese competitors. Growth has slowed by historic standards – it was 9.3 per cent in the 1960s, 10.3 per cent in the 1970s, 7.7 per cent in the 1980s, 6.3 per cent in the 1990s and 4.4 per cent post-Millennium – but South Korea has not suffered a recession since 1998.

While international attention focused on crisis and recovery, developments were under way below the radar, for in the 1990s South Korea had taken a radical approach to IT. Like its industrial transformation, its high-tech miracle would be top-down. Government led the way, providing funds, subsidizing technology and co-operating with companies to create infrastructure; firms then created the services and products to run on it. Korea's first mobile phones had been imported for Olympic management. When it came to establishing a network, Seoul technocrats realized that, if they adopted existing formats, they would be playing catch-up. Instead, Korea became the first nation to adopt and commercialize Code Division Multiple Access (CDMA), created by US venture Qualcomm. It was a bold decision. Europe and the United States had adopted different standards, meaning that Korea would be globally out of synch – but could run better services. A triopoly of carriers ensured competitive pricing; the first service came online in 1996.

In 1993 government officials had heard Al Gore talking of the 'Information Superhighway' and decided that South Korea needed one. All new office and residential buildings were embedded with fibre-optics. Competition among carriers, the country's small land area and the fact that 65 per cent of Koreans lived in apartments, accelerated speed of wiring. By 2005 the entire country had broadband coverage. Connection speeds were four times faster than in the United States, and soon 30 per cent of global Wi-Fi hotspots would be in South Korea. It was probably the world's finest national Internet backbone.

The country was hailed as a living IT test lab. Tech royalty such as Bill Gates visited. Business boomed: carriers KT and SKT ran services, manufacturers Samsung and LG sold gadgets, while 'PC Bangs' (high-speed Internet cafés) proliferated. New companies – Internet portals Naver and Daum, game developer Nexon – joined Korea's list of top firms. But South Korea had always been poor at capitalizing and incubating small companies and there had been excessive promises and over-exuberance. The venture industry was snuffed out amid the credit crisis.

This left the big boys to profit from the tech boom and another infrastructure boom. Incheon International Airport, on a reclaimed island in the Yellow Sea, opened in 2001; it has won seven international 'world's best airport' awards. In 2004 the KTX, a bullet train based on France's TGV, started running. However, the last Park-style infrastructure vision – a grand canal – was downgraded to a linkage of Korea's four main rivers. Designed to kick-start a leisure/tourism boom in South Korea's interior, its implementation between 1998 and 2004 was flawed. Amid environmental and corruption concerns, it failed to match its vision.

Surviving *chaebol* had exited the crisis stronger. Previously, as chips-to-ships conglomerates, they had been 'me-too' metal bashers, leveraging high volumes and low prices. In 1998 they refocused on core competencies rather than doing everything. Previously, companies had been hardware-centric; now interest rose in the softer side of business. Samsung Electronics imported Korean-Americans to work on marketing; Hyundai Motor Group imported German designers. R&D spend shot up. In 2001 *Businessweek* wrote, 'Enough of the Hyundai Jokes.' By the mid-noughties, Korean products were aspirational and Korean companies were household names. The *chaebol* had emerged as global brands.

Yet none is a 'blue ocean' innovator: no Korean company has yet invented a new product category. Their 'second mover' strategy obviates the investments made and risks taken by 'first movers'. Instead, *chaebol* forge up extant pathways with their fast decision-making, efficient manufacturing and global distribution. While not inventors, they are incremental innovators, registering huge numbers of patents – thinner displays, faster chips, devices with more applications. Apple's patent lawsuit against Samsung in 2013, which won it US$890 million in damages, suggests that South Korean companies still have IP issues. But it also granted Samsung credibility, by demonstrating that even its mightiest rival is wary. And *chaebol* never shed their economy of scale. Currently, Samsung Electronics is the world's largest electronics company, the biggest seller of memory chips, smartphones and TVs, and number two in semiconductors. LG Electronics is the world's largest display maker; Hyundai Heavy its top shipbuilder; and Hyundai Motor its fifth biggest automaker.

Foreign investors in South Korea often fail to grasp the quirks of the local business environment, for Korean capitalism was never a free-market variety. Internally, it was a centrally planned, state-led, producer- rather than consumer-centric model. Externally, it was assisted by ex-colonizer Japan and Cold War ally the United States, which provided, respectively, US$5 billion and US$5.5 billion of the US$12.8 billion in aid that South Korea received between 1945 and 1995. Its driving force was global trade. But the overriding factor was sweat equity: both state and companies were top-down machines that brilliantly (if ruthlessly) leveraged manpower. And even if it is an unfamiliar model, its result is undeniable: development succeeded beyond all expectations.

Twenty-first-century South Korea provides a benchmark for 'rags-to-riches' development. The world's fifteenth largest economy and seventh-largest exporter (ahead of the UK and Russia), it is home to world-class companies, infrastructure and technology. Given that the country was poverty-stricken, inexperienced in global trade and home to not a single global brand in the 1960s, this is remarkable. Koreans overuse the term 'economic miracle' – but they cannot be accused of exaggeration.

Cyberspace and shamanism

In the very heart of Seoul, hidden by high-rise apartments and clinging to the lower slopes of Mount Inwhang, among sacred stones and streams, lies a tiny village of temples: Kuksadang, the national *mudang* (shaman) shrine.

Shamanism is Korea's native religion, and its roots sink both deep and wide. Even in the twenty-first century, shamans command high prices for such services as fortune-telling, good-luck rituals and exorcisms, while elements of shamanism have infiltrated Buddhism and Christianity. Koreans were never great explorers of the outside world – the windows of traditional homes, built around courtyards, face inwards, not outwards – but shamans enter different dimensions, converse with spirits and undertake quests without physical travel.

Koreans' enthusiastic adoption of IT is usually explained by its cutting-edge infrastructure and world-class tech companies, but cultural factors are at play, too. Koreans are communal and education-obsessed and IT is both communication enabler – explaining higher numbers of personal gadgets – and education enabler – explaining high numbers of home PCs. The mentality is egalitarian-but-competitive: if Kim has something, Park and Lee want it, too. Hence, Koreans upgrade personal gadgetry with dizzying frequency. Moreover, hangeul is tailor-made for digital devices: it reads vertically and horizontally.

Korea's cyberscape is renowned. Seoul City provides a global benchmark for e-government. Social networking sites Cyworld and I Love School predated Facebook. Game designers are world-class and are pioneers in monetizing free games by selling online gear, avatars and advertising. It is even therapeutic: after a 1999 fire killed 23 elementary schoolchildren, a web designer provided parents avatars of their deceased children, which they could take for outings in a bucolic virtual landscape.

There is a dark side. Obsessive online gamers have tracked down and assaulted competitors offline. A couple's baby died while they obsessively gamed (ironically, their game involved rearing a virtual child). A 2011 government survey found that 2 per cent of Koreans needed game addiction treatment, and everyone under 16 is banned from gaming between midnight and dawn.

Does cyberspace enable Koreans' inner shamans? Perhaps. Online role-playing games provide different dimensions; Internet chat rooms enable conversation with strangers; online malls take users on quests (even if for something as mundane as a new shirt). Still, online fanatics might heed a warning from Korea's original virtual voyagers. The most perilous task a shaman can perform is to enter a trance, descend into hell and rescue a lost spirit. This kind of psychic SAS operation comes at heavy cost: some elite *mudang* have a shaky grip on sanity.

3

Political miracle

'No one saves us but ourselves,
No one can and no one may,
We ourselves must walk the path...'

Buddha, *The* Dhammapada

▶ Whisky and bullets

Evening, 26 October 1979. In a safe house near the presidential mansion, President Park dined with close associates. Ribs were grilled; Chivas Regal flowed. Discussion focused on an ongoing crisis: unrest in the south. Cha Chi-chol, the thuggish paratrooper who handled Park's security, suggested a harsh crackdown. KCIA head Kim Jae-kyu differed. Discussion grew heated. Kim excused himself, then returned to the banquet, pistol in fist. 'How can you govern with a worm like this?' Kim asked Park, gesturing at Cha. He fired. Cha fell, mortally wounded. Then Kim took aim at Park.

Many Koreans would have happily levelled that gun that night. Park, always authoritarian, had become dictatorial. In 1972 he enacted the 'Yushin' ('Rejuvenation') constitution, granting himself major powers and dissolving re-election limitations. That year, he was elected unopposed. In 1974 Park's wife, a softening influence, was shot by an assassin aiming at her husband as he delivered a speech. (Park insisted on finishing his speech. His wife died.) He became increasingly closeted, his security apparatus increasingly brutal. In 1975 eight anti-Yushin activists were executed. Park recognized his unpopularity: Koreans, he wrote, would 'spit on his grave'. In 1978 Park was (again) elected unopposed. Now riots were under way in the city of Masan, where students had joined labourers – a worrying alliance for the regime. But Park's nemesis came from within.

Point blank, Kim fired. Park, bloodied, slumped. 'Your Excellency, are you all right?' gasped a serving woman.

'I'm fine!' Park snarled. Then silence. After 18 years of rule, the engineer of industrialization was dead.

Park was buried in a state funeral; Kim was hanged. It is unclear whether he planned a takeover or had simply fired in anger. Prime Minister Choi Gyu-ha assumed the presidency. It was a golden opportunity. In 1961 South Korea had been undeveloped, but Park had laid a solid foundation. Now, would political development catch up with economic? Choi lifted some of Park's most repressive measures. Politicians debated a new constitution; labour confronted management; citizens discussed a previously taboo subject – politics. Meanwhile, a stocky, balding general was investigating the KCIA's role in Park's death.

▶ 'Please remember us'

Chun Do-hwan's command background was military intelligence and special forces. He had served in Vietnam and headed a secret army faction, composed largely of fellows from his military academy class. Chun froze the KCIA's budget, cowing that feared agency. In December, suspicious that he and his faction were about to be sidelined, Chun arrested the army's chief of staff. This granted Chun de facto control of the military. In April 1980 he became KCIA head. In May he told the cabinet he was taking power. Martial law was declared nationwide. Students protested; troops hit the streets.

The strongest resistance rose in the south-western Jeolla Province – the seat of the Baekje Kingdom and traditionally rebellious. In the nineteenth century it had incubated the Donghak Rebellion and was the holdout of the last Korean War partisans. More recently, Jeolla had been left out of industrialization: Park had sited most major industrial plant in the south-east. This was as far as possible from North Korea (traditional invasion corridors run down the peninsula's western flank), but it was also Park's, and Chun's, personal political base. Regional discrimination was rife.

Chun deployed 'black beret' airborne rangers to Gwangju, Jeolla's provincial capital. On 18 May their aggressive *choongjung* ('True Heart') riot-control tactics proved excessive: a deaf man was killed. Infuriated citizens rallied. Reinforcements were summoned; ten ranger battalions were soon in action. By 20 May they faced perhaps 100,000 incensed demonstrators. As decontrol loomed, the 'black berets' opened fire. Protesters responded, seizing guns from police stations and armouries; the demonstration became an uprising. On the 21st, the rangers retreated and a citizen's committee took over Gwangju. But Chun would permit no city to rebel. The army blockaded communications, regrouped and reinforced. On 26 May, units from five divisions converged on the city. Armed protesters prepared. Two females in a jeep broadcast a poignant loudhailer message: 'Please remember us!' Rangers advanced on Provincial Hall where the uprising's hardcore had deployed for a last stand. They were annihilated. After five days of defiance, Gwangju had fallen in a 90-minute operation.

For most Koreans, details were scant. Seoul asserted that a communist rebellion was under way and, amid

Political miracle

a press blackout, even the US Embassy was in the dark; only a handful of foreign reporters covered the tragedy. But, as facts emerged, Koreans were furious. Questions still hang over numbers but, according to Gwangju sources, 154 citizens were killed, 76 disappeared, and over 4,000 were wounded or arrested. The 'Gwangju Massacre' would become Korea's Tiananmen Square. In June, Chun dissolved the National Assembly. In August, Choi resigned and Chun started mass arrests; some 60,000 persons would be dispatched to 're-education camps'. That month, Korea's electoral college declared Chun president. There was no other candidate.

▶ Seoul perfume, skull cops and black buildings

Chun's political rivals were the 'Three Kims': Kim Young-sam ('YS'), Kim Dae-jung ('DJ') and Kim Jong-pil ('JP'). YS, from the powerful political base of Busan in the south-east, had opposed both Rhee and Park. DJ, a left-leaning figure from Jeolla, had nearly beaten Park in the 1971 election; in 1973 he was abducted by the KCIA, bound, taken aboard a boat and was about to be cast into the sea when the US CIA intervened, saving his life. After Gwangju, DJ was sentenced to death by Chun; Washington and the Vatican intervened; he was imprisoned rather than executed. In 1961, then a colonel, JP had assisted Park's coup and founded the KCIA. Park made him prime minister, but removed him in 1975.

The Three Kims would prove no brake on Chun: in 1981 he made political parties illegal – apart from his own. The media was strictly controlled – the president was always the first news item – and the KCIA beefed up. Meanwhile, the United States remained supportive of a Cold War ally with a growing economy: Chun was welcomed in Washington by US President Ronald Reagan. But, although Chun had castrated politics, dissent was brewing.

In South Korea, students are known as 'the conscience of the nation'. In Joseon, literati had traditionally protested unjust policies by memorializing the throne, and students led the 1919 Independence Movement against Japan and demonstrated against Rhee and Park. As the 1980s proceeded, they would form a telegenic vanguard of resistance against Chun. After Gwangju, the army was not called out; instead, students faced a massive, 150,000-strong riot police force.

Korea's top universities were in Seoul; these campus districts became battlegrounds. Armoured black vans, with multiple grenade launchers on their roofs, unleashed barrages of tear-gas. Convoys of riot police buses – dubbed 'chicken coops' for their wired-up windows – raced to block streets, channel protests and disgorge policemen. Formations of police in samurai-style body armour and helmets (attire poorly designed to make Koreans look favourably upon its wearers), hefting rectangular shields and wielding sword-like batons, manoeuvred under walkie-talkie command. On their flanks lurked the feared 'Paekkoldan' ('White Skull Cops' – named after their white helmets): martial arts-trained snatch squads, in denim and lightweight armour, who targeted ringleaders. Students fought back with poles, stones and petrol bombs. Most wore face scarves to hide their identifies, and coated their nostrils with toothpaste to counteract the gritty, peppery tear-gas – 'Seoul perfume' – hanging over the city.

For foreign photo-journalists, snapping the action through fogged-up gas masks in the front lines, the scene looked chaotic, furious: the waves of students crashing into and receding from police shield walls, backlit by bursting Molotov cocktails and clouded in smoky haze, resembled battles from the Three Kingdoms. Yet there were limits, lines not crossed. Police were forbidden from entering campuses, and (mostly) this rule was observed. When police, singly or in groups were captured, they were not brutally handled. Student percussionists often drummed, creating a festive *shinpparam*. Former protester Ryu Jung-hee recalled good-natured cops calling a student to come and recover her shoe, which had come unlaced during the scuffle, and lay between the lines. Another female protester found threats to 'tell her parents' of mistreatment were enough to win her release: harassed police could do without extra paperwork. Attractive female protesters were sometimes asked out by their captors: many cops were students taking a study break to do their two-year national service. And, of course, no official wanted another Gwangju: their own children and grandchildren were students.

Even so, for the ringleaders there was much to fear. Activist Park Jeong-chol, 21, discovered this when he was grabbed by plain-clothes policemen on the night of 18 January 1987 and taken to Seoul's Namyeongdong district, to be interrogated on the whereabouts of other activists. Perhaps he wondered why the building, in a backstreet, was matte black and featureless. Perhaps he wondered why its fifth floor had no windows, only slits. Perhaps he wondered why Cell 509, behind its green steel door, featured a fully fitted bathroom (complete with faux-marble tub), a prominent electric socket and walls insulated with wood.

The black building, situated close to Seoul's US Army base, and the KCIA HQ at the foot of the picturesque Mount Namsan, were notorious. Waterboarding and shock treatment were the preferred methods of torture, but savage physical cruelty was also used: a lawyer named Roh Moo-hyun was horrified to meet two clients missing toenails. One Namyeongdong detainee, Kim Geun-tae, suffered so severely that, years after his torture in 1985, he could visit neither doctor nor dentist: clinics bought on post-traumatic stress disorder. (Kim, a prominent politician in the 1990s, died in 2010 from torture complications, aged 64.)

Park would discover the reasons for the bath, the electric sockets and the wooden walls that muffled screams. But we cannot know what he thought, for he did not survive his treatment: he was the first student to be killed by the authorities since Gwangju. When a Catholic association – the priesthood was another hotbed of protest – broke the news on 18 May, the police explanation for Park's death was, 'He drank a cup of water and died of shock when a policeman banged his hand on the table.' The derisive response suggested that the police considered the public dolts. And Park's case was particularly poignant: he had been a poor boy who had managed, by dint of hard work and intelligence, to enter the elite Seoul National University.

What made the torture particularly disgusting was the fact that, while Seoul certainly was threatened by Pyongyang, it had little to fear from a protest movement that was incapable of sparking revolution. The movement had lost faith in the United States after Gwangju. Protesters believed that Washington had permitted Chun to manoeuvre army units – a belief that was strengthened when Reagan met Chun. Previously, liberal America had been revered; the Carter administration was often at odds with Park, and Washington had demanded leniency for both YS and DJ. In December 1980, anti-Americanism reared its head when the US Information Service in Gwangju was torched; in 1985 students occupied Seoul's USIS library. Hence, the protest movement looked to the United States' enemies for a competing ideology. Students shifted leftward – in some cases, radically . But their timing was off: they were embracing socialism just as average Koreans were starting to enjoy the prosperity delivered by capitalism. While many Seoulites were irked by the inconveniences caused by endless demos, they indulged students for opposing a despised president. But, in ideological terms, hardcore demonstrators were out of synch with wider society and offered no alternative political vision.

▶ People power

Public anger over Park's death simmered; a memorial protest was called for 10 June. On 9 June a protester, Lee-han Yeol, was severely injured by a tear-gas grenade (he died weeks later). On the 10th, Chun (with execrable timing) nominated Roh Tae-woo as his candidate for the December election. Roh, a general who had aided Chun's takeover, was considered a shoo-in: another dictator. A civic group called for demonstrations to demand true democracy – one man, one vote, rather than the electoral college system Park had established.

The response was extraordinary. Cities were overrun with protests, but something was different: reporter Mike Breen, driving through a demonstration, realized that these protesters were not students. He watched a businessman whacking riot cops with a briefcase; when they bundled him away for a beating, a crowd of *ajummah* – Korea's formidable matrons – intervened; the cops backed down. Salarymen and housewives demonstrating? This was middle-class revolution. The regime was under intense pressure: if bloodshed occurred, the 1988 Olympics might be called off. The situation was on a knife edge. On 29 June, Roh conceded.

The first fully democratic election since Park implemented Yushin in 1972 would be held; the Three Kims were allowed to return to politics. Campaigning was hectic, with DJ – a famed orator – addressing crowds of tens of thousands. But Korean politics had always been less about ideology and more about regionalism, factionalism and powerful leaders. DJ and YS could not agree on a single candidate. Meanwhile, Roh could assuage conservative fears of North Korea (whose agents underwrote such fears by blowing up

Political miracle

Korean Air Flight 858 in November, killing 115), leverage his new democratic credentials and talk up the soaring economy. On 16 December 1987 the people voted. The opposition split; Roh won.

Yet the election was an extraordinary achievement. Customarily, Korean political change had been top-down: dynastic overthrows, foreign takeovers, coups d'état. Now, after centuries of monarchy, three and a half decades of colonialism and four decades of authoritarianism, transformation had been bottom-up: average Koreans had activated true democratization. In summer 1988 South Korea hosted the Seoul Olympics. Some observers were shocked by the country's fierce nationalism, but most were impressed by the economic muscle underwriting the impeccably managed games.

In retrospect, iconic photographs of the 1980s are misleading. Shots of troops patrolling Gwangju, students battling riot police or DJ haranguing massive rallies suggest that these forces delivered democracy. They did not. For all the sacrifice of Gwangju citizens, the gutsiness of student demonstrators and the righteousness of opposition leaders, they were, in the end, just contributors. The transformer was the bourgeoisie: only when the middle class rose was democracy attained. There is little to admire about Chun, but his acceptance that force was no longer feasible merits praise. Unusually for a dictator, he stepped down without a bloodbath; his bow to 'people power' was arguably his greatest achievement. He is likely to be South Korea's last dictator.

Today's Koreas exemplify the 'Kirkpatrick Doctrine' (named after a key thinker in the Reagan administration), which asserts that, however odious rightist authoritarian regimes are, they are less stable, and therefore more susceptible to change, than leftist totalitarian regimes. As a case in point, protest overthrew Seoul's junta, but 'people power' is non-existent under Pyongyang's iron fist.

In today's South Korea, one holdover from the authoritarian decades is suspicion. Many South Koreans, having experienced right-wing dictatorship, still distrust right-wing administrations. Conspiracy theorists opine that North Korean attacks are scaremongering tactics engineered by shadowy right-wing forces in the south, while hard leftists, who protested against Seoul's dictatorship, decline to criticize Pyongyang's harsher version. Conversely, 'red-under-the-bed' thinking is still current among some rightists – but, undeniably, Pyongyang did support anti-Chun activism.

Activist Kim Young-hwan believed in North Korea: he distributed subversive literature and was imprisoned in the 1980s. He was subsequently taken by submersible to Pyongyang for training, where he met Kim Il-sung himself before being re-infiltrated in the South. But his beliefs would change. In 2012 he was imprisoned in China for conducting anti-North Korea activities. Back in Seoul, he told the media that the reason China had been harsh was that they understood his skills at undermining governments: he had been trained by Pyongyang.

Such 'blowback' may concern Pyongyang spymasters, but they have a greater irony to consider. Pyongyang backed anti-Chun forces and protest overthrew right-wing dictatorship for good: another coup is unthinkable. This leaves Pyongyang with no popular force to support south of the DMZ. Democracy has obviated revolution.

▲ Protester Lee-han Yeol is supported by fellow students after being struck by a tear-gas grenade during the demonstrations of June 1987. Over 1 million South Koreans attended his funeral the following month, and he has remained an iconic figure in the country ever since.

▶ Football, 'F**king USA' and mad cows

Post-1987, democracy continued apace. Roh forged ties with the Soviet Union, China and Eastern European countries. He was succeeded in the Blue House by former oppositionist Kim Young-sam, who joined the ruling party to run on its ticket. Under YS, the dominant symbol of Japanese colonialism, the Government General Building in central Seoul, was demolished and a high-tech national backbone was laid. Kim Dae-jung took power in 1998 as the first opposition president. He mastered the economic crisis, enacted a bold 'Sunshine Policy' of engagement with North Korea and banned tear-gas. Although there had been mass demonstrations when YS joined the governing party, street politics dissipated considerably in the 1990s. But in 2002, when South Korea co-hosted the World Cup with Japan, Koreans would, again, hit the streets en masse.

The Seoul Olympics had showcased South Korea to the world, but in 1988 the nation was still unsophisticated, parochial and chauvinistic. When the sporting world returned to Korea 14 years later, it would not just be impressed, it would be charmed. By 2002 Korea had exited a devastating financial crisis and was building a reputation as a high-tech wonderland and exporter of music, film and TV drama. Koreans themselves were more internationalized, but what would astonish observers was their communal passion. While official events were pre-planned with typical Korean precision, what happened on the sidelines (which became the big story) was spontaneous. As the Korean squad – hitherto a World Cup also-ran, but now enjoying a hometown advantage – advanced to the semi-finals, 'Red Devils' (Korean supporters, named after their red strips) flooded downtowns nationwide to watch games on giant electronic displays. They came in their millions; the Cup became a huge street festival. Commentators had seen nothing like it, and, unlike many international sporting events, with their violent tribal rivalries, this was inclusive: overseas visitors joined the fun, wearing Korean colours. International media were won over; some compared Korea favourably to Japan. Of course, for old-timers, 2002 echoed 1987; *shinparram* apparently compelled Koreans to mass, emotive displays. And more was to come after the football finished.

In the 1980s, anti-Americanism had been ignited by Washington's support for Chun and, in the early 1990s, by pressure to open Korean markets. In 2002 young Koreans were more Americanized in their taste, dress and outlook than their parents, but less pro-American; meanwhile, the George W. Bush administration differed with Seoul over North Korea policy. In February a Korean skater had been disqualified at the Winter Olympics, granting an American victory and igniting Korean fury; the same month, Seoul's American Chamber of Commerce was occupied and trashed by student radicals. In June, a US armoured vehicle killed two Korean schoolgirls in a traffic accident. Remorseful GIs held a candlelit vigil at the crash site, but US Forces Korea was always a lighting conductor for public anger – partly due to its high profile, partly due to bilateral agreements placing it beyond Korean law. During the Cup, Korea was quiet, but afterwards, when the responsible GIs were acquitted in a court martial, there was a sense that Korean sovereignty was undermined, its demands disrespected. Local reporting was accusatory.

Hundreds of thousands gathered with candles in Seoul. Giant US flags were torched. A song, 'Fucking USA', was chanted by popular singers (including a chubby rapper named Psy). A US embassy staffer was speechless upon meeting a group of nuns whose charity projects the embassy sponsored: they sported 'Fuck USA' badges. A restaurant sign reading 'Americans Not Welcome' made international news. Young GIs were abducted by students on a subway and forced to 'apologize'; another GI was stabbed. Americans were stunned; a general was filmed in tears. Compounding US shock was the lack of rage directed towards Pyongyang; on the day of South Korea's last World Cup match, North Korean gunboats had initiated a naval clash, killing six South Korean sailors.

Demonstrations coincided with the presidential election. The left-leaning Roh Moo-hyun – boosted by a last-minute mobile phone 'get out and vote' campaign – won, partly quelling public anger. A self-educated, down-to-earth human rights lawyer, Roh was South Korea's first 'everyman' president; he had no military or (long-term) political background. The right-wing National Assembly reacted badly, impeaching Roh for minor electoral law violations. He was acquitted by the Constitutional Court. In subsequent Assembly elections, the conservatives lost seats. Roh continued Kim's engagement with Pyongyang and people were – depending on viewpoint – horrified or delighted when he publicly corrected President Bush during a press conference on North Korea. But Roh also deployed troops to Iraq and brokered a Korea–United States free trade agreement. However, he was too sensitive for politics, taking media criticism personally and publicly wondering why he had taken the job.

In 2008 the next president, Lee Myung-bak ('MB'), was a poster child of Korean achievement: poor and too thin to do military service, he had joined Hyundai and worked his way to become CEO of construction before entering politics (reportedly, after realizing that he could not reach the summit at the family-run *chaebol*). MB's victory overturned a decade of left-wing rule. The Left reacted. When Lee, currying American favour, permitted the reimportation of US beef (earlier banned due to 'mad cow' fears), crowds – part-inspired by an alarmist, inaccurate documentary – hit the streets. Protests started in a carnival atmosphere, but morphed into hardcore anti-government demonstrations and eventually fizzled. As president, MB worked to ramp up the economy, carried out his grandiose 'Four Rivers' project and ignored North Korea. An angry Pyongyang responded with deadly attacks.

In 2012 South Koreans voted again. The Right's candidate was Park Geun-hye – Park Chung-hee's daughter. The election became almost a referendum on her father. Park won narrowly, her main supporters being, ironically, the generation that had lived through the Park years and remembered him as a nation-builder; younger voters considered him a dictator. Other key electoral issues were left-driven: 'economic democratization' – a protest against the power abuse of the *chaebol* – and the creation of a welfare system. How Park will meet these challenges remains to be seen, but the demands of the latter are already stretching budgets.

Post-election, news broke that the National Intelligence Service (NIS, the KCIA's successor) had employed cyber spies to influence citizens to vote for Park. The Left demanded a non-partisan investigation; some called for nullification of the election. Roh's impeachment, 'mad cow' protests and the NIS scandal point to an odd trend: after each of the last three presidential elections, the losing side has attempted to overturn the results.

▶ Quiet streets, noisy parliament

South Koreans' favourite exhortation, accompanied by pumped fist, is the (English) word 'Fighting!' Modern Koreans are intensely competitive, nowhere more so than in politics. In most democracies, politics is the 'art of the possible' – of debate; of compromise. In Korea, although the two main parties have moved closer to the ideological middle ground in recent years, the National Assembly often resembles a mosh pit rather than a debating chamber.

A starting point in CIA analyses is: 'Where does the power come from?' The Assembly makes laws and is elected every four years. The two main parties are the right-wing Saenuri Party, the descendant of Park's political machine, and the Democratic Party, the descendant of DJ's party. (The left wing, echoing Korea's endless battle between orthodoxy and heterodoxy, dub themselves 'liberals' or 'progressives', but are more conservative than the right wing in certain areas: they tend to be more nationalistic and less inclusive. It is the right wing that placed a German-born Korean at the head of the Korean Tourism Organization and a Philippine-born Korean in the Assembly.) The single-term president governs via ministries and is elected every five years. The Assembly is unicameral, so, if a party loses a vote, it has no recourse to an upper chamber. And if one party controls both Assembly and Blue House, the opposition is left out in the cold.

This makes Assembly politics all or nothing, hence the brawls and even tear-gas releases in the chamber, as lawmakers desperately try to prevent voting. Likewise, parliamentary walkouts and sit-ins are common. Partisan squabbling delays legislating: 2013 marked the eleventh straight year in which the Assembly passed the budget in the early hours of New Year's Eve. This does not bespeak careful, thoughtful lawmaking.

Outside the chamber, grassroots democracy remains strong, as witness endless small, though noisily disruptive, demonstrations outside corporate, media and government offices. But the emotional mass protests that once defined Korean politics have dwindled: 2008 saw the last big ones. This may be because students no longer demonstrate. In the fast-growth 1980s, students were virtually guaranteed jobs after graduation; in today's mature economy, with slower growth and higher youth unemployment, students need to study. Moreover, Korea has a low unionization rate and farmers' struggles against globalization (a force that enriched Korea) look unwinnable. Finally, Korea's raucous cybersphere, a furiously excitable forum, may have sucked energy from the streets. Even so, Koreans' delight in emotional gatherings suggests that we have not seen the last big demos: in recent protests, a new banner – 'The Demo Party' – has been spotted.

Seoul's houses of horror have gone. Namyeongdong is now the Police Human Rights Commission; Park's cell is a shrine. The Namsan KCIA Centre is a youth hostel. In 2007, speaking on the twentieth anniversary of his son's death, Park's father said that he feared modern Koreans were forgetting the sacrifices democracy demanded. Perhaps – history, a contentious subject in Korea, is very poorly taught. Yet disinterest in political processes and distrust of politicians are quixotic, but common, features of democracies. To see a polity where leaders are worshipped, Seoulites need only gaze north.

South Korea's worst job?

In the United States and the UK, retired leaders are respected figures who undertake select political/diplomatic missions or charitable activities, sit on company boards, and earn coin as public speakers. Not in South Korea.

Rhee Syngman died in exile. Park Chung-hee was assassinated. Chun Do-hwan and Roh Tae-woo found themselves in court in 1997, charged with mutiny and treason; their key interrogator, in a trial that electrified the nation, was the then-firebrand lawyer Roh Moo-hyun. Chun was sentenced to death and Roh to life imprisonment. (Both were pardoned by outgoing President Kim Young-sam on the advice of incoming President Kim Dae-jung.)

After leaving office, YS saw a son jailed for corruption. DJ picked up a Nobel Peace Prize for his daring engagement with North Korea, but suffered indignity when it was revealed that his groundbreaking summit with Kim Jong-il had been secretly enabled by a half-billion dollar payment to Pyongyang. Roh Moo-hyun and his family were probed on corruption charges immediately after he left office: three months later, Roh committed suicide. That sparked national shock and a reappraisal of his legacy: he is now considered Korea's most beloved ex-president.

Lee Myung-bak appears to have escaped intact. Current President Park Geun-hye has approved another probe into

Chun's affairs; his family have since been required to sell a number of assets.

That South Korea's ex-presidents are held to account by their publics is encouraging and democratic: it will hopefully discourage future bad behaviour in the Blue House. But it raises the question of why the job is so coveted...

Social miracle

'After hardship – happiness'

Korean proverb

▶ Koreaphobia

I first visited South Korea in 1989 and lived in the country in the early 1990s. At first sight, the nation was unwelcoming. Design, even aesthetics, seemed absent: Seoul was grey, square, spartan; cars were boxy and black, white or grey.

People dressed like clones. Men's fashion was particularly gruesome, remarkable for obtrusive belt buckles and chunky tie clips (sometimes embedded with faux gems). The first thing I saw on Korean TV was a bulky, 40-something gent with short, spiky hair and a boxy black suit growling aggressively at the screen. A gangster movie? No: a fashion icon. Women looked better, but faced perils: a crone waddled around downtown armed with a switch to thwack the legs of girls in short skirts.

Not only did people look the same but they also seemed to think the same. Unless it was a domestic political or regional issue under discussion, Korean A might say, 'We Koreans think this...' and Koreans B and C would likely agree. Children, asked their ambitions, would answer 'businessman' or 'housewife'.

Gentility was absent. In public, people barged into each other without apology. Driving was a mêlée of jockeying and honking, and hawking and spitting were de rigueur.

In a country where work was all, play opportunities were limited. If you asked a Korean his or her hobby, the popular answer was 'Sleeping!' The leisure sector was primitive; shopping and nightlife offered limited options;

and, beyond fast-food franchises and hotel restaurants, Western cuisine was invisible.

Diversity was non-existent. With many believing that the Uruguay Round (1986–94) global trade talks were a plot to prise open Korea's market, imported products were seen as unpatriotic. The winning essay in an English-language newspaper contest was an explication of the writer's distaste for mixed-race children. Children mockingly chanted 'Hello, Mr Monkey!' at foreigners. In this nationalistic, male-dominated society, a Korean woman dating a foreign man might be cursed, spat at or worse. A friend told me (earnestly) that just one homosexual, 'officially licensed' to loiter on US Army bases, lived in Korea.

The foreign community was small and isolated. Diplomats and businessmen considered Korea a 'hardship posting'. Besieged in pubs in Itaewon, Seoul's foreign quarter, expatriates – businesspeople, GIs and English teachers – whined endlessly about their host nation.

▶ Koreaphilia

Today South Korea is almost a different country. Seoul's architecture remains undistinguished, but a handful of iconic structures have risen, quirky designs for everything from bus shelters to public toilets have sprouted and the city's grey palette is splashed with blue and green.

Appearances have undergone radical upgrades. South Koreans are among the best-booted-and-suited people in the world – and some of the best-looking. The male fashion icon has shifted from the aggressive, 40-something hardcase to the cheery 20-something metrosexual; the patrolling witch with the switch would now have far too much bare flesh to thwack.

Opinions and aspirations have expanded. Not everyone wants to work for a *chaebol*; children have wider hopes and dreams. Public manners have improved. Driving is still a battle and urban areas remain packed, but those jarring pedestrian collisions are no more, and theatrical hawking and spitting have diminished.

Play opportunities have exploded – from jet-skiing on Seoul's Han River to skiing in winter mountain resorts. Seoul and Busan offer some of Asia's (ergo, the world's) most incendiary nightlife, with international party-goers from Hong Kong and Shanghai jetting in for frenetic weekend breaks.

The import stigma has evaporated, and diversity has increased in every direction. Koreans are enthusiastic sporters of international brands and cities buzz with foreign-style bars and restaurants. Mixed-race marriages are common and mixed-race children are now widely considered appealing rather than unattractive; Seoul even boasts a lively gay scene.

The foreign community has expanded. Residence and recreation choices are no longer restricted to expatriate ghettos, and Seoul has climbed up the desirability ranking for companies and embassies. Resident foreigners' attitudes seem to have shifted from Koreaphobia to Koreaphilia.

This revolution in looks, behaviours, attitudes and lifestyles got going in the 1990s – a decade that would be for Korea what the 1960s had been to the West; an era of generational shift, new ideas and new freedoms. It would blossom fully in the 2000s.

The prime change agent was democratization. Social and cultural life had been stunted for decades under dictatorial governance, so a renaissance was inevitable once oppression lifted. Another was prosperity: in 1980, per-capita income was US$1,598; in 1990, US$6,147; in 2000, US$10,841; in 2011; US$22,489. Amid anti-consumption attitudes and policies, the middle class had been savers, not spenders. Once change came, increased demand expanded consumer choice. An accelerating factor was the 1997 financial crisis and subsequent pick-up of IT, which bypassed traditional, top-down media, enabling trends and developments to be disseminated and communicated with ever-greater speed and breadth.

▶ Globalization, multiculturalism, liberalism

Exports had long been South Korea's key earner, but in hierarchical Korean companies the number of executives who travelled abroad was relatively low. Special permission (or connections) had been required for males to travel overseas for pleasure, study or business. Only in 1989 were passports widely issued; subsequently the Kim Young-sam administration preached *segyewha* (globalization).

Koreans responded. The first wave that flocked abroad in high-visibility tour groups of predominantly middle-aged Koreans would become the bane of international airlines. Noisy, clumsy, rude and even smelly (many carried pungent *kimchi* overseas), they were dubbed the 'Ugly Koreans'. But another group was also exercising their passports. Youthful Koreans were both travelling independently and enlisting for overseas study – at schools, universities, graduate schools – in soaring numbers. By the Millennium, Koreans made up the third largest population of foreign students in the United States after China and India (nations with much larger populations). They bought home new ideas, attitudes and tastes.

Customarily, Koreans considered themselves happily homogeneous. This belief, combined with anti-Americanism, could see foreigners being treated with suspicion or hostility. But, once Koreans started flocking abroad and online (a medium that opened a two-way window on to the world), the belief in 'foreign otherness' cracked. Back home, the trend manifested in a plethora of foreign restaurants and bars opening to suit the tastes of newly cosmopolitan Koreans, while the country's most notorious food item lost popularity: Koreans are today far more likely to own dogs than consume them.

Meanwhile, the expatriate community was expanding in three distinct groups. First, globalizing Koreans needed to learn English, a demand that propelled an influx of thousands of young Anglosphere graduates to South Korea. Many settled, worked for Korean firms or opened small businesses. Secondly, with newly prosperous

Koreans reluctant to work in low-tech factories, hundreds of thousands of Third World workers flooded in as labour for small manufacturing businesses. Thirdly, in the increasingly urbanized 1990s and noughties, Korean farmers found it difficult to attract local spouses, leading to a surge in 'mail order' brides from China and South-east Asia: by 2006, 11 per cent of marriages were bicultural; by 2020, 5 per cent of children are expected to be biracial. This trend means that South Korean multiculturalism is being birthed in rural, rather than urban, areas – the opposite of the Western experience.

Indications are encouraging. While Third World workers, brides and biracial children do face discrimination, such incidents are covered by sympathetic media, and NGOs have sprung up to assist them. Foreign-born Koreans now sit in the National Assembly, and foreigners appear in entertainment media. Today, foreigners are more likely to be greeted with a smile than with a shoulder bump, while Korean children prefer to politely practise English than mock aliens. It is increasingly common to see Korean men dating Western women (rather than simply Western men dating Korean women, as was the case in the recent past), suggesting liberalized attitudes towards both gender and race: society is becoming less male-centric, more open.

Gender identities are in flux. Women don't do military service (two years), so they spend more time in education and enter the workforce earlier than males. Their knowledge and financial independence, plus exposure to international gender mores, has helped overturn traditional expectations for women: marriage and childbearing. Males have become correspondingly more accommodating, but marriage and birth rates have plummeted. Democratization may explain why aspirational male icons are young meterosexuals rather than macho and middle-aged: the latter personifies authoritarianism. To grossly simplify: Korean women have become more 'masculine' in behaviour and attitudes; Koreans men have become more 'feminine'.

Formerly taboo sexualities are emerging. Seoul's expatriate quarter of Itaewon, with its mosque, foreign businesses and international mores, is where Koreans have traditionally fled to experience a freer social environment. Itaewon's sexual geography has diversified. Its red-light district, 'Hooker's Hill' (which originally served GIs), has been joined by 'Homo Hill' (aka 'Brokeback Hill') and even a transvestite zone, 'Tranny Alley' – more openly gay scenes than existed before.

▶ Consumerism, beautification and quality of life

In the early 1990s the South Korean media brimmed with outraged reports of the so-called 'Orange People'. This urban tribe inhabited Gangnam, a brash suburb that rose from paddy fields south of the Han River in the 1970s, as Seoul expanded. Many Gangnamites became real-estate millionaires overnight, and their nouveaux riches children scandalized Korea by spending big on foreign brands. The 'Orange People' were, in fact, pioneers. The economic miracle had granted Koreans spending power, but it was only after 1997 that Koreans were actively urged to spend, in order to inject liquidity into a crisis-hit economy. Koreans were once known for knock-off brands; now, expanded spending power and greater fashion consciousness make them among the most brand-centric people on earth.

Similarly, they are strikingly good-looking. This urge to beautify is due not simply to increased consumer choice, but also to the groupthink – 'I have to keep up with the Kims' – and competiveness – 'I have to be a winner' – that rack Korean society. With the economy maturing and youth unemployment climbing, young Koreans can no longer expect to walk into a job. So – assuming lack of connections – how to beat the competition? Korea has no class system, so accent and surname are irrelevant. Koreans are highly educated, so unless they graduate from the elite SKY (Seoul, Korea, Yonsei) universities, qualifications deliver little competitive advantage. This leaves appearance, which may explain why Koreans are among the biggest consumers of plastic surgery on earth. In 2005 the BBC estimated that 50 per cent of Korean women in their 20s had cosmetic surgery; in 2014 Korean men purchased 30 per cent of the global market for male moisturizing products. It also explains why Koreans are so trendy, even if their fashion retains elements of conservatism – dyed hair is about as outré as it gets; grunge, Goth and punk looks are largely absent.

Beautification extends beyond people. Seoul – the national trendsetter – is becoming increasingly liveable. A landmark change was undertaken by Lee Myung-bak. As Hyundai Construction CEO, Lee had built a massive elevated expressway over Seoul's Cheonggyecheon stream – virtually an open drain – in the 1970s. As Seoul's mayor in 2002, Lee tore down the expressway and regenerated the 5-kilometre (3-mile) stream in a US$900-million project that gave central Seoul a facelift. Unlike previous infrastructure projects designed to promote growth or raise facilities for international events like the Olympics, Cheonggyecheon aimed simply to upgrade locals' quality of life. That initiative was followed by the creation of an inner-city forest and riverside and mountain-side park complexes that have dyed a once-grey city green. Lee, however, overreached himself. As president in 2008, he attempted to link Korea's four rivers. He was out of touch with environmental trends, for, while Cheonggyecheon had removed concrete, the Four Rivers project added it. In the face of environmental and corruption concerns, it failed.

In hard-working Korea, leisure and tourism were considered frivolous for decades. But implementation of the five-day work week in 2003, bespeaking changed attitudes, led to upgrades in the sector. Leisure options range from *jjimjilbang* (luxurious, inner-city sauna and spa complexes – an evolution of the Japanese-style bathhouses that existed in every neighbourhood in the days before Korean homes had bathrooms) to Cineplexes to temple stays. Leisure spending has risen, propelled by groupthink. For example, hikers outfitted to conquer Everest – Gore-Tex clothing, expedition boots, high-tech alpenstocks – will be seen on even the gentlest trails. Under authoritarian governance, a midnight curfew was in place, but today's nightlife has rebounded: it is now 24/7, its intensity magnified by city zoning that encourages the conglomeration of bars and clubs in pulsating, neon-lit, downtown clusters.

Lifestyle was irrelevant between the 1960s and 1980s; in today's South Korea, it is central. Like many foreigners, I feel more comfortable with the nation's younger generation, with their internationalized outlooks and behaviours. However, the earthier, pushier, rougher-edged, 50- and 60-something Koreans sacrificed everything to build their country from nothing: they are Korea's greatest generation.

Korea's new-looking old buildings

Be it cars, clothes or possessions, the old, worn look does not sell: Koreans don't drive vintage cars, wear retro clothes or (God forbid) use last year's digital gadget. In a country energized by competitive pressure, everything is up to-the-minute and this includes buildings – particularly 'old' historic ones. Confused?

While the Japanese colonial government restored Buddhist temples, it dismantled Seoul's palaces, turning them into parks and zoos. War further devastated traditional heritage, leaving Korea with few iconic landmarks. Latterly, major restorations (often complete reconstructions) have transformed historical sites. The result is that fourteenth-century palaces, 600-year-old city gates or medieval walls look brand spanking new for good reason: they are. While such 'restorations' are ersatz, they look magnificent: South Korea has invested heavily in monumental architecture.

Alas, in a hierarchical society, there have been few related efforts to preserve humbler architecture. *Hanok* (traditional, one-storey Korean cottages) were razed nationwide in the name of 'modernization' as Koreans flocked to apartments in the 1980s. (Koreans raised in *hanok* in the 1950s and 1960s recall them as uncomfortable and inconvenient, but *hanok* can be easily fitted with modern kitchens and bathrooms today.) Likewise, the ambient, narrow alleys that once defined Korean cityscapes have disappeared; blocks of monotonous office buildings and apartments have taken their place.

One antique residential district in Seoul, Bukchon, has been designated a 'preservation zone', but most original *hanok* there have been destroyed and replaced with modern ('renovated') copies. Many are empty show homes owned by the rich, making Bukchon a strangely empty neighbourhood. Compare this to Europe, where old homes and inns are carefully renovated and used for their original purposes, rather than becoming empty, museum-like showcases.

Korea's dreary urban aesthetics result from rushed development, vertical construction packing more people into less space, real-estate owners seeking maximum rental returns, and architecture being classified as science, not art. They are also a by-product of relentless future-focus. This attitude is a national strength; the downside is that most urban architectural heritage has been bulldozed. It markets itself as a city where old meets new, but Seoul's heart is broken.

▶ The Korean Wave

Prior to the late 1990s, Korea's most prominent cultural export had been a method of kicking people in the face. Korean masters who learned karate during the colonial era branded their art *taekwondo* ('way of foot and fist') in 1955 and emphasized kicking techniques, the standout feature of the near-extinct Joseon martial art *taekkyun*. Taught to soldiers, taekwondo went global during the Vietnam War, with GIs proving enthusiastic martial-arts students both in Vietnam and in Korea. (Among the latter was an airman named Chuck Norris, who would showcase Korean boot-work in 1980s martial arts thrillers.) In the United States, Americans and a motivated cadre of expatriate Korean masters established taekwondo studios, while Seoul took taekwondo global. Spectacular high kicks, unseen in other martial arts, made taekwondo a hit; the first world championship was held in 1973.

With the national flag prominently displayed, taekwondo had been promoted as an ancient Korean art, so when the original martial art of *taekkyun* (dubbed a cultural asset but not officially promoted, it had come within one master of extinction) underwent a surprising renaissance in the liberalized 1990s, things could have proved embarrassing. But, by then, taekwondo had moved on. Its governing body had astutely repositioned it as a modern, global sport. It made its Olympic debut in 1988 and is today a programme event. Taekwondo is among the world's most popular participation sports – especially in developing nations, for it requires zero equipment – and is probably the most recognized Korean word worldwide.

Taekwondo was a zero-to-hero success story. Why were other art forms not popularized globally? Partly because taekwondo, a physical practice, presented no linguo-cultural barriers. Moreover, martial exports were appropriate fits for martial regimes – regimes that censored popular culture. Things would change after democratization.

In 1999 Chinese media coined the term *'Hallyu'* ('Korean Wave') to describe excited local responses to a Korean boy band, H.O.T. The same year, an inter-Korean action thriller, *Shiri*, shattered Korean attendance records before grabbing number-one spots at the Japanese and Hong Kong box offices. And *Autumn in My Heart*, a tear-jerking soap opera, had Korean audiences bawling – a reaction repeated in China, Hong Kong, Singapore and Thailand. What were the wellsprings of this new-look Korean content?

Among Koreans studying overseas in the 1990s were attendees at film schools in the United States and Europe; they brought new skills home. New foreign influences also had an impact on music. In the 1980s pop musicians were largely crooners and anti-government-focused rock, blues and folk artists. The South Korea of the 1990s was a brighter, happier nation. Local musician and DJ Lee Soo-man watched MTV in the United States and bet that the combination of bright, pretty stars and video content would work in Korea. Yang Min-suk had been exposed to hip-hop by African-American GIs in Itaewon nightclubs and became a dancer in Seo Taiji and the Boys, an influential band of the early 1990s. In 1996 Lee launched SM Entertainment and Yang launched YG Entertainment. They would become Korea's top talent agencies.

Their output was more upbeat than previous pop, but their business paradigm was all-Korean. They used a formulaic, almost industrial manufacturing process; hard training and hard work were paramount. Recognizing that the local market was too small to earn big, particularly after digitization undercut CD sales in 2006, they focused on exports. The difference between industrial manufacturers and Wave-makers was that the former had been assigned sectors by government; the latter acted on their own initiative.

Political developments spurred the Wave. In 1996 the Constitutional Court deemed censorship unconstitutional, opening broad new fields for artists. Thrillers could take on North–South themes and humanize an enemy that state propaganda had, in the past, portrayed as having horns. (While Korea has not birthed a local-specific genre like Hong Kong's kung fu theatre or Japan's samurai epics, North–South thrillers, combining action and tragedy, are a staple.) In 1998 a long-standing ban on Japanese cultural imports was overturned while the nation's screen quota system – which reserved a percentage of screens for local films – came under US trade pressure. These developments increased overseas competition.

The 1997 crisis upended the traditional entertainment industry: old players went bankrupt while companies like CJ and Orion Entertainment focused more aggressively.

CJ and Orion launched Cineplex chains, making them producer-distributors and creating a bigger ticket market. Moreover, key artists of the 1980s – film-makers like Im Kwon-taek and singers like Han Desu – had been artists first and foremost. In the late 1990s, backed by commercial companies, artists were more populist.

Technology enabled content. The advent of cable TV in South-east Asia created demand for new programming. Early Korean soaps were Japanese lookalikes, so Korean producers, like their industrial forebears, undercut Japanese rivals on price to build market share. Also, Korean products did not suffer the historical stigma that Japanese products faced in Chinese markets. Subsequently, web-savvy Korean stars bypassed traditional distribution networks and went global by embracing social media.

From the Millennium, the Wave rolled across Asia. In 2002 syrupy melodrama *Winter Sonata* captured the hearts of Japanese matrons, earning male lead Bae Yong-joon the honorific 'Yonsama' and making him a superstar. For the first time, Koreans – traditionally discriminated against – won popularity in Japan. Japanese enjoyed Korean products for their retro quality, but for China and South-east Asia, 'Cool Korea' – with its gorgeous stars, gorgeous locations and high technologies – was aspirational. In 2003 a historical soap, *Daejangeum* ('Jewel in the Palace'), became a hit region-wide. SM produced bands like HOT, SES, BoA and Girls Generation; YG rolled out Big Bang, G-Dragon and Se7en. They sang catchy songs, were gorgeous in appearance and could dance like the dickens. Unlike grungy Western popsters, they (and TV soaps) were wholesome: sexy but hardly raunchy. These cultural characteristics appealed to Asian marketers as well as Asian markets. Soon, Korean stars were not only creating music, they were endorsing products and doing commercials. Rigorous training enabled many singers to go cross-platform, appearing in TV, films and musicals, cross-fertilizing the Wave. From the get-go, savvy management packaged stars as brands.

However, the sector of the Wave that generates 80 per cent of cultural content revenues is not film, TV or cinema: it is computer gaming. Gaming has been less hyped within Korea, perhaps because its products do not look intrinsically Korean – but this factor helped it cross language and culture barriers for overseas players.

Video-game saloons had been a popular escape for study-stressed children in the 1980s. In the 1990s official censorship and poor business practices by importers killed the Japanese gaming-console market. So Korean designers, leveraging the new IT infrastructure, focused on online games, a format that appealed to local children (who could play while pretending to study on home PCs). It was further propelled by communalism: mass multiplayer online games enable groups of allies to form, and can bring hundreds of thousands of players online at once. Popularity led to the creation of leagues, corporate sponsorship and teams, even offline stadia. Companies like Nexon and NCSoft published epic games like Raknarok, Lineage and Mu as well simpler, free-to-play games like Kartrider and Maple Story.

▲ 'Gangnam Style' presented a new-look, fun and funky Korea to the global public, while Psy burnished the national brand by replacing Kim Jong-il and Kim Jong-un as the world's most recognizable Korean

While South Korean music companies innovated new revenue models – such as selling cellphone ringtones and tunes for personal homepages – game firms pioneered sales of in-game products, skills and ads.

South Korean films are generally edgier than pop and soaps and a handful – noir thriller *Old Boy* (2003), winner of the Jury Prize at Cannes, and the Buddhist parable *Spring, Summer, Winter, Fall and Spring* (2003), an art-house hit – won Western attention. But while formulaic pop and melodramatic soaps have captured niche audiences in Western markets, the Wave was largely an Asian phenomenon until summer 2012. Then a chubby, comically dressed rapper uploaded a YouTube video of his latest song, a mocking take-down of Korea's most pretentious district. Psy was popular in Korea but no A-list star; no local pundit expected this idiosyncratic artist – the antithesis of carefully marketed, by-the-numbers teen bands – to go global. But his video, featuring top TV comedians, a zany dance and the addictive refrain 'Gangnam Style!' became the most watched YouTube clip ever. Having studied music in the United States, Psy spoke English and adroitly bounced from viral to mainstream, appearing on TV shows worldwide, visiting the UN Headquarters and even addressing the Oxford Union.

His success extended beyond music. Pre-Psy, the most recognizable Korean faces globally had been those of North Korea's dictators. Their replacement by Gangnam's affable son was an unexpected boost to South Korea's global image – an image very much on the public mind.

▶ Brand Korea

Park Chung-hee had cultivated South Koreans' hunger for success, and three decades after his death they retain a desperate urge for overseas recognition. Local media feverishly report international rankings of everything from educational achievement to corruption; endless articles express anxiety about a possible downturn in the Wave; and for years a major downtown store displayed pictures of Nobel Prize winners with a prominent empty space for the first Korean. Underlying all this is a sense that South Korea does not receive due international respect.

There is some substance to this. It is a universal fact that perceptions lag behind altered realities, and for decades dominant images of the peninsula had been grim: war and devastation; joyless industry-scapes; militaristic leaders; chaotic riots; threatening North Korea. Post-1997, South Korean conglomerates hired international marketers to upgrade their brands. Via global ads, PR, endorsements, sponsorships and product placements, it worked: in 2005 Samsung's brand value famously overtook arch-rival Sony's. With corporate branding understood, Koreans began wondering why the national brand lagged.

Government had done much to boost Korea's image, hosting high-profile international events: the 1988 Olympics, the 2002 World Cup, the 2005 APEC Summit, the 2010 G20 Summit and the 2018 Winter Olympics (won by Pyeongchang after a never-say-die third bid). For such events, no expenses are spared to ensure that facilities are tip-top, programmes run smoothly, and opinion leaders are well treated: reporters covering the World Cup enjoyed free massages, acupuncture treatments and city tours.

But, while facility construction and event planning are core strengths of Korean bureaucrats, overseas marketing is not. Some wince-worthy promotional campaigns have been undertaken by governmental organizations unfamiliar with English or global marketing norms. The capital was branded 'Hi Seoul', Korean mushrooms were advertised as 'romantic' and an award-winning brand created by an international agency for Incheon Airport, 'The Winged City', was dropped.

Equally problematically, non-governmental organizations waded in. Disingenuous campaigners promote Korean food not as tasty – which it certainly is – but as healthy – which it is not. (Unlike Anglosphere diets, Korean cuisine does not cause obesity, but its heavy pickled, salted and spiced content gives Koreans the world's highest stomach cancer rates.) Nationalistic NGOs and individuals strive to lure a disinterested United States on to Korea's side in territorial and historical disputes with Japan by running poorly written ads in global newspapers and other media spaces. International organizations have been bombarded by emails demanding they use the Korea-preferred term 'East Sea' along with the accepted English term 'Sea of Japan' for that body of water. These tactics are lauded in Korea, but whether they upgrade or degrade the national image is questionable.

Fortunately, amateurish marketing is increasingly irrelevant: the ever-improving national 'product' is organically upgrading the national 'brand'. South Korea's flagship firms generate income and respect for the country, while the Wave generates interest and affection. Koreans are well educated and hard-working, and since globalizing in the 1990s, increasing numbers have won positions and fame worldwide: LA Dodgers pitcher Park Chan-ho; Manchester United footballer

Park Ji-sung; UN Secretary-General Ban Ki-moon; and entertainers too numerous to mention. The Wave drives tourism to Korea, and Korea lies between two of the world's biggest tourist markets, China and Japan. All this creates collateral interest in Korean cuisine, the 'Korean look' – many tourists undergo plastic surgery, based on the mugs of Hallyu stars – even Korean literature. Leveraging its unusual position as a highly developed nation that was, within living memory, desperately poor, Seoul tutors developing countries in Korea-style development economics and dispatches Korean volunteers around the developing world.

In short, since the late 1990s South Korea has developed a formidable soft-power portfolio to supplement the industrial hard power it has been growing since the 1970s.

Hermit Kimdom

'In this world, if you close your eyes, someone will cut off and eat your nose.'

Korean proverb, warning of the evils of the world

▶ From Kim I to Kim III: communism to monarchy

On 8 July 1994, shocked South Koreans braced for change in the North: Kim Il-sung, at the age of 82, had died of a heart attack and the prevailing wisdom had it that Kim's son lacked the legitimacy to take over. In fact, the transition proved almost seamless. Kim's son would weather the worst catastrophe North Korea had endured since the war, before passing power to his own son. The unprecedented mutation of communist state into de facto, third-generation monarchy is yet another surprise Korea has sprung upon the world.

In 1953 North Korea lay devastated: just two buildings remained standing in Pyongyang. Yet it had the lion's share of Korea's natural resources and Japanese-era industry; with aid from the Soviet bloc, it rebuilt swiftly. Kim's war-making had led his people to disaster, so Kim's media rewrote reality, asserting that South Korea and the United States had ignited the war and portraying Kim as victor. In another falsification, *juche* ('self-reliance') was promoted as Kim's ideology (conveniently ignoring Pyongyang's dependency upon foreign allies and assistance). Tellingly, few North Koreans can recite Kim's great thoughts, but he is revered – for Pyongyang's propaganda machine formulated the world's most powerful, pervasive personality cult.

In 1945 this had got started in typical Stalinist style as Soviets positioned Kim as the new leader; in the mid-1960s, in part-response to China's Cultural Revolution, it was massively reinforced with statues, pictures and stories that sometimes went to ludicrous extremes: Kim, 'The Great Leader', had killed Japanese while still an infant and could dispatch several enemies with one bullet. (In his writings, Kim himself expressed embarrassment at some such beliefs.) Propaganda also demonized the United States and promoted the purity of the Korean race. In the 1970s a new myth came into focus. Kim's son had been born in the USSR, but state media insisted that he entered the world atop Mount Baekdu (an iconic, extinct volcano on Korea's China border) during his father's guerrilla campaigns. Kim, suffering from a tennis ball-sized neck tumour (never shown in photographs), and possibly suffering intimations of mortality, had decided on a familial power-transition; it was made official in 1980. Why?

After his mentor Stalin was besmirched after his death, it seems that Kim wanted to preserve his legacy. To ensure that, he needed someone entirely trustworthy to assume command. Moreover, Koreans revere family and for millennia Korea's leaders had been familial monarchs. Easing the transition was a total absence of potential contenders. Kim's personal power base was his guerrilla comrades from Manchurian days, but there had been other factions: Soviet Koreans from the USSR; others who had operated with Mao; and other Manchurian guerrillas who had not been with Kim's group. Kim purged them all. There is believed to have been resistance to family inheritance inside the state's key power guarantor in 1994, so, for added insurance, Kim's son bought the loyalty of the army by replacing *juche* as the pre-eminent state watchword with *songeun* ('military first': prioritization of the armed forces).

The 'Dear Leader', Comrade Kim Jong-il, lacked his father's common touch: while Kim I had frequently mingled with citizens, Kim II was a virtual hermit who gave 'on-the-spot guidance' at factories and bases and clapped regally for cameras, but never delivered a public speech. (Though once, excited during a military parade, he ad-libbed, 'Long live the glorious Korean People's Army!') Unlike his father, a chum of East Germany's Erich Honecker and Romania's Nicolae Ceauşescu, Kim II did not socialize with other leaders, and barely travelled. A film buff, he preferred being behind the camera rather than in front of it – an appropriate location for someone directing the vast film set of state. He loved luxury, importing fine cognacs, sushi and pizza, and maintaining yachts and palaces. He and top cadres enjoyed a troupe of female 'entertainers' recruited from beauty contests. (After servicing top elites, the girls were married to second-tier cadres – army officers or journalists – but forbidden to discuss their previous activities.) Kim II's combination of secretiveness, odd appearance (pudgy figure, bouffant, zip suits) and threatening policies (human rights abuses, strategic weapons programmes) made him ideal fodder for global media, a dictator both sinister and ridiculous – a living 007 villain.

In 2008 Kim's good living caught up with him: he suffered a stroke. 'Pyongyangologists' in Seoul detected the elevation of his son Kim Jong-un. When Kim II died in December 2011, the succession was secure: Kim III played the leading role in a brilliantly staged state funeral. (Kim II was subsequently stuffed and displayed in a mausoleum beside 'eternal president' Kim I.) With his PR-friendly leadership, black tunic and sidewall hairdo, Kim III seemed to be modelling himself on his revered grandfather. He spent his first year reshuffling key figures in the party and military. Compared to his bizarre father, the grinning young man, with his Swiss education, appeared a breath of fresh air. But the transition from Kim II to Kim III had been rushed: just three years, compared to the decades-long progress from Kim I to Kim II. Behind his throne was believed to be a 'regent', Jang Song-thaek, an experienced party operator who had married into royalty by wedding Kim II's sister. Jang was executed two years into Kim's reign.

▲ Like father, like son: Kim II (right) and Kim III (third from right) observe a military parade in central Pyongyang, 2011.

The world was aghast – both at the death of a high-level official, and because Kim had culled his own uncle. In fact, purges were a feature of North Korean politicking, and inter-familial killings had been a feature of Joseon. The real reason for the execution of Jang, 'the richest man in North Korea', remains opaque. Propaganda said he was plotting a coup, but there are other theories. One: he amassed personal wealth and power at the expense of the army (which plays a major economic as well as military role). Two: Jang was maintaining contacts with Beijing, and Kim's estranged half-brother Kim Jong-nam lived in exile in China; perhaps (the theory goes) Kim III believed that Beijiing and Jang were plotting to replace him with Kim Jong-nam.

How can the Kims' North Korea be defined? It is not communist – Pyongyang officially dropped references to communism in its constitution in 2009 – but is an odd conglomeration of influences. Demands for worship of a single 'god' and some propaganda iconography resemble Christianity. (In the 1920s and 1930s US missionaries considered Pyongyang the most Christian city in Korea.) North Korea is socialist in word but its economy has been largely capitalist in deed since the Millennium. Its race-based rhetoric resembles Nazi Germany's; its personality cult recalls Mao, Stalin and Hitler. With its bloodline inheritance, behind-closed-doors decision-making, reliance upon a close elite and 'Hermit Kingdom' mentality, North Korea closely resembles the Joseon Dynasty. (This is an analysis underwritten by the country's name. In English, it is informally 'North Korea' and formally 'The Democratic

People's Republic of Korea/DPRK', but in Korean it is 'Joseon' – the modern dynasty retains the name of its ancient forebear.) However, old Joseon was neither militaristic nor ultra-nationalistic, and did not foster a personality cult. The final model, combining the Kims' god-king status with the regime's anti-foreign paranoia, ultra-nationalism and 'military-first' policy is Imperial Japan, meaning that North Korea looks similar to the regime Koreans most love to hate. (Nationalism on both sides of the DMZ shrouds this uncomfortable analysis.)

Kim's military lacks the regional ambitions and expeditionary capabilities Hirohito commanded, but guarantees his regime. With no opposition existing either locally or abroad, Kim III, who will be 30 in 2014, could feasibly be in power in the 2040s. He appears more economically focused than his father and perhaps more risk-tolerant: in 2013, while Seoul and Washington conducted annual military exercises, Kim launched a rhetorical offensive that shook the world with its vitriol, extreme even by Pyongyang standards. State media roared that nuclear war could break out, that the 1953 armistice was nullified. In fact, that agreement was already badly holed.

▶ War without end

17 January 1968. They crossed the DMZ at midnight; 31 shadows, elite North Korean special forces. Their destination: the presidential Blue House, 35 miles south. Their mission: the assassination of Park

Chung-hee. With the president dead, North Korea would initiate an ambitious operation: key installations and communication networks would be seized by thousands of infiltrating commandos; citizens would rise; South Korea would fall.

Among South Korean hills, the commandos were spotted by four loggers, who were swiftly captured. Kim Shin-jo, the unit second-in-command, suggested executing them; his commander decided to bind and leave them. The commandos moved out; the loggers freed themselves and sounded the alarm, triggering a huge search operation. However, the North Koreans moved cross-country so swiftly that they were already beyond the search cordon. On 21 January they lay up, overlooking Seoul. The city was swarming with troops, so the commandos took a bold approach: concealing weapons under their coats, they simply walked into the city. Just minutes from the Blue House, they were challenged at a police checkpoint. An intense running battle broke out; the commandos scattered; a huge manhunt was launched. All the North Koreans were killed, bar Kim, who surrendered, and another, who disappeared; 66 South Koreans and three Americans died.

The assassination bid had failed. On 23 January, North Korean naval units seized the spy ship USS *Pueblo* in the Sea of Japan. Seven days later, communist forces launched the 'Tet Offensive' in Vietnam; and throughout 1968–9 North Korean special forces skirmished with South Korea's deniable operations unit, the Headquarters Intelligence Detachment (HID), in the DMZ. There is no evidence that Pyongyang and Hanoi co-ordinated

1968's attacks, but, given their military co-operation during the Vietnam War, it is certainly possible.

The year 1968 remains the bloodiest since the 1953 armistice, but the North's 'asymmetric forces' have been widely engaged since. In the 1970s four infiltration tunnels were discovered under the DMZ. In 1983 commandos blew up the Korean cabinet during a state visit to Rangoon, narrowly missing President Chun Do-hwan. In 1987 spies bombed a South Korean airliner, killing 115. Commandos kidnapped Japanese citizens to use as language trainers for spies, and in 1996 a mini-submarine ran aground on South Korea's east coast. Its commandos attempted to fight home overland; all were killed.

Subsequent action shifted to the Yellow Sea and the Northern Limit Line (NLL), the maritime frontier never officially agreed to by Pyongyang during the DMZ armistice negotiations. The NLL shields several South Korean islands close to the North's coast, and covers lucrative crab-fishing grounds. In 1999 and 2002 patrol boats clashed fatally in this area. In 2010 the South Korean corvette *Cheonan* was sunk with the loss of 46 sailors. A South Korean–international investigation named a North Korean torpedo the culprit, but Pyongyang denied involvement. Later that year North Korean artillery shelled the South Korean island of Yeonpyeong, killing four.

Pyongyang's attacks in the pre-democratization years seemed designed to overthrow the Seoul government and achieve unification. The objectives of the latter attacks – including 1976's axe murders, in which two US soldiers were killed while cutting trees at Panmunjeom – are less clear. These – bar 1996, which looks like a reconnaissance gone wrong – have featured regular, rather than special, units. The patrol boat combats could be territorial clashes, though the 2002 attack, on the day of South Korea's last World Cup game, appears deliberate. Moreover, North Korea wants to dissuade Seoul and Washington from carrying out exercises and may even use attacks to grab international attention.

There is a more worrisome explanation. In a nation of 23 million, North Korea's 1.1 million-strong military must justify its size, status and privileges. Few believe it could conduct another 1950-style invasion, but it can posture threateningly and launch sudden, limited attacks – difficult for Seoul and Washington to counter without risking escalation. Military threats and even nuclear tests barely affect Seoul, where – contrary to excited global media headlines about 'rising tensions' – life continues as normal and capital markets barely fluctuate. However, military tensions may be useful for Pyongyang to unify its own populace – focusing their attention away from local shortcomings towards foreign threats. If internal rationales drive attacks, there is little the outside world can do to prevent them; the only solution is to vow harsh retaliation – Seoul's stance since 2010. (And no attacks have occurred since.)

The year 1968 still resonates. In Pyongyang, the *Pueblo* is moored as a tourist attraction/propaganda monument. (Its crew was released after 11 months of harrowing imprisonment.) In Seoul, the mountain behind the Blue House remains heavily garrisoned. Ex-commando Kim, who surrendered and turned, is a pastor. And his comrade who disappeared? In an incredible feat of soldiering, he made it back across the DMZ: Kim spotted him on TV in the1980s, a be-medalled general accompanying Kim Jong-il during a televised parade.

▶ Famine, capitalism, information breach

Pyongyang's eroded but formidable army – the perfectly choreographed drill of North Korean soldiers puts the US Marines and Brigade of Guards to shame – camouflages the degradation of the state. South Korea's GDP overtook North Korea's in the early 1970s. Then, the fall of European communism in 1989 and the collapse of the Soviet Union in 1991 lost Pyongyang privileged trade and aid. State-owned industry (the only kind) was already uncompetitive; now plants and power stations clunked to a virtual halt. Meanwhile, serial floods and crop failures devastated an agricultural sector that, due to foolish policies and mountainous topography, was always precarious. The state distribution system, which fed the public, broke down. In the mid-1990s North Korea was gripped by terrible famine.

Smuggled photographs depicted emaciated peasants in dusty fields; feral orphans begging in dilapidated towns; corpses rotting on barren riverbanks. Reports leaked out of meals of tree bark – even human flesh. Hundreds of thousands fled to China. Yet so closed were North Korea's doors that international bodies had no clear picture. In 1995 Pyongyang requested external assistance, but aid agencies were hampered by disintegrating infrastructure, travel restrictions and officialdom that prevented supervision of aid distribution. It is estimated that 500,000 to 1 million people (out of a population of 22 million) died in 'The Arduous March' and malnutrition has stunted North Koreans, who are, on average, 2 to 6 centimetres (1-3 inches) shorter than South Koreans.

Famine led pundits to anticipate (again) North Korea's collapse. Not only did it not collapse, but desperation initiated economic transformation. There had always been some state-authorized markets in North Korea, but in the 1990s survival markets began sprouting everywhere (a process similar to South Korea's wartime markets). Cross-border trade increased as frontier controls with China were relaxed. A new class of entrepreneurs, familiar with supply and demand, market pricing and currency trading – many markets in North Korea accept won, yuan, dollars and euros – emerged. Illegal Chinese cellphones enabled cross-border communication. With capitalist activity 'unofficial', corruption was necessary for the new economy to operate; it became rampant. Some entrepreneurs employ officials, such as border guards, in their distribution networks. Yet the new middle-class capitalists required powerful patrons to permit and protect their operations, so traditional elites also profited. And there have been some reforms: in 2013, Pyongyang allowed farmers to keep a certain proportion of their crops, rather than handing them all over to the state, and is busily establishing carefully insulated foreign investment zones. Since famine eased at the end of the 1990s, numerous official attempts have been made to dampen capitalist activity – unsuccessfully. An apparent currency reform in 2009 was badly handled, wiping out people's savings and further diminishing a discredited regime in the eyes of its citizens.

Amid famine, North Koreans traded for food and medicine. Post-famine, they developed an appetite for entertainment and information, creating a thriving trade in smuggled media in DVD, CD and thumb drive formats. Previously, information channels and content were state-controlled: newspapers and TV. North Korea state TV offers three channels, including one running foreign programmes such as wildlife documentaries, sports events, even royal weddings. (Defectors are surprised to discover that a popular cartoon with a revolutionary theme – *The Stupid Cat and the Wise Rat* – is actually American: *Tom and Jerry*.) Pyongyang's information monopoly is no more. In particular demand among smuggled media is South Korean material, from soap operas to Psy. Its subversive potential is part-undermined by changes in state propaganda. Pyongyang no longer claims that South Korea is poor; instead, it asserts that the proud North is a 'pure' Korea, free of alien influence and US 'occupation'. Similarly, South Korean and US assistance has been portrayed not as aid but as tribute.

China, always wary of border instability, stepped in to assist North Korea after the collapse of the USSR with food and power aid. It is the largest investor and trade partner, running an approximately US$1 billion annual surplus that North Korea looks unlikely to repay – making the surplus a de facto subsidy. A handful of non-Chinese firms in North Korea are engaged in tourism, animation, diamond cutting, gold mining, textiles and cell-phone operation, but major international companies, concerned about political risk and reputational risk, and dissuaded by crumbling infrastructure, lack of rule of law and UN sanctions, stay clear. Even so, vitalized by market economics and Chinese trade and aid, North Korea's economy is rising: South Korean data suggests that from 2000 to 2012, the country saw eight years' growth, four years' recession. Pyongyang – with its empty boulevards and lack of bustle – once provided a relaxing contrast to other Asian capitals, but recent visitors note new prosperity: retail choices, high-rise apartments, stylish people, improved power supply and even (minor) traffic jams.

Pyongyang runs Intranet and mobile telephone systems, though these are as much vehicles for oversight as freedom: both channels are believed to be monitored, and cellphone subscribers, around 2 million, correspond broadly with the 10 per cent of the population making up the capitalist middle class with ties to the elite, and the elite themselves. (Top cadres also have a dedicated cell-phone network.) Internet access is highly restricted, and foreigners who use it – aid workers, diplomats, businessmen – know they are monitored. Reluctance to implement significant reforms on the Chinese model remains for several reasons. Establishing a tax system would obviate state appropriation but would also contradict the sacred legacy of Kim I and anger an already

Hermit Kimdom

unhappy populace. Liberalizing communications, such as travel (both national and international) and Internet access, could undermine regime control.

The traumatic 1990s transformed North Korea. Change, once top-down, is increasingly bottom-up. Communism has been ditched as too difficult to achieve, but while North Korea remains constitutionally socialist (i.e. there is state control of productive assets), its economy is largely capitalist. Propaganda remains pervasive, but smuggled external media has breached the state's information barrier. 'Real' walls are also cracking. Rising trade and corruption have made the China border porous, easing defection.

▶ Defection, control and the gulag

The early trickle of defectors, pre-1990s, escaped largely for political reasons. They included Hwang Jang-yeop, a close aide to Kim I and the main author of *juche*; a cousin of Kim II also arrived. (North Korean agents in the South made unsuccessful assassination attempts on Hwang, but managed to kill Kim's cousin.) One of Kim I's bodyguards defected after seeing preparations for the handover to Kim II. Knowing that Stalin had lost a son in World War II and that Mao's son had been killed in Korea, he was disgusted by Kim's favouritism.

Since the late 1990s greater numbers of defectors have arrived in South Korea, mostly fleeing starvation and poverty. In South Korea, new professionals have emerged: 'brokers' (often ex-defectors) who help Northerners escape in return for payment. These, and Christian missionaries, courier defectors along the 'Underground Railway' out of North Korea, through China to Mongolia or South-east Asia, and eventually to South Korea. Despite the deprivations of North Korean life, overall defector numbers are tiny: just 26,124 North Koreans came South between 1953 and 2013.

It is impossible to estimate the extent of North Korean thought control. For some, the Kims are gods. 'From the moment we are born, we hear "Kim Il-sung" and "Kim Jong-il"; we learn their names before our parents' names,' said defector Lee Hyeon-seo. 'I didn't think they drank, smoked, married or used toilets.' Many defectors cannot bring themselves to criticize the Kims, choosing, instead, to blame knavish bureaucrats for North Korea's woes. (A similar situation pertained during the Third Reich's collapse: many Germans blamed party officials rather than the Führer.) On the other hand, members of North Korea's most motivated special units – survivors of the 1968, 1983 and 1987 attacks – have turned after capture. And recent defectors say that few now believe in a state that takes rather than gives – offering free food, housing, education and medicine pre-famine, North Korea could once legitimately claim that its citizens had 'nothing to envy' – but are compelled to go through motions of loyalty. Many defectors turn to Christianity – perhaps as a substitute for Kim worship.

As it is incredibly dangerous to cross the DMZ, most defectors flee over the China border. One reason for low defection rates is the difficulty of exiting not just North Korea – often as simple as bribing a guard and wading a river – but China, which forcibly returns defectors/refugees. Another is inability to organize and communicate, for regime oversight is insidious. This is carried out not only by means of the police, secret police and state security: ordinary North Koreans, too, are required to regularly report activities of members of their own households to officials. Then there is fear. North Koreans know the end game for certain crimes: firing-squad executions are public. And in a secretive state with no due process for 'political crimes', the threat of the midnight door-knock hangs heavy, for, though few know what goes on inside 'labour', 're-education' and 'total control' camps, they know that people, even whole families, disappear.

In 2007 a speaker at the Seoul Foreign Correspondents' Club received an unusual request: he was asked to remove his trousers. His name was Shin Dong-hyuk and he claimed to have escaped from North Korea's most notorious facility: 'Total Control Camp 14'. Shin's tale was so extraordinary that he was asked to present evidence of his escape over an electrified razor-wire fence. Shaking slightly, he did so: his legs were a tracery of scar tissue. Shin had been born in the camp, for North Korea routinely punishes not only perpetrators but also their families. In this perverted world, Shin informed on his own mother, who was planning to escape. She was executed; Shin, far from being rewarded, was horribly tortured. A hook was hacked into his groin, his skin scorched. Shin's suffering was extreme, but not unique. Other escapees report inmates dying of starvation, beatings, drowning in latrine pits – even vomiting blood after eating cabbages coated with biological agents. Repatriated defectors pregnant with babies of Chinese parentage have reportedly suffered forced abortion, in line with the state's 'pure blood' ideology.

This is not the full picture of a system incarcerating an estimated 200,000 men, women and children: some inmates undertake nothing worse than agricultural work, and 2014 judicial reforms permitted family members to bring inmates in certain camps food. But North Korea's notoriety as a human rights abuser is earned – as is its reputation as a rogue state.

▶ Strategic weapons, sunshine and sanctions

In 1994 the ageing Kim I, seeking improved international relations and reduced tensions, met ex-US President Jimmy Carter. On the agenda was denuclearization. In the early 1950s Moscow had assisted Pyongyang with nuclear research, and in 1965 a plutonium-based power reactor was constructed at Yongbyon. In 1991 US forces announced the withdrawal of nuclear warheads from South Korea. That year, UN inspectors claimed North Korea was refusing full access to Yongbyon, raising suspicions that the plant was producing weapons. In October 1994, three months after Kim's death, Washington and Pyongyang signed the 'Agreed Framework' under which the international community would provide North Korea with civilian light-water nuclear reactors and fuel aid; Pyongyang would mothball Yongbyon's plutonium programme. It was a promising plan. Work started on the reactors, but political squabbling in Washington and expectations that North Korea would collapse led to delays in aid delivery. Pyongyang's faith in US promises withered.

In 1998 Kim Dae-jung (DJ) took office in Seoul. There had been periods of inter-Korean détente in the 1970s and 1980s, but Kim proposed a bolder plan: 'The Sunshine Policy', based on Aesop's fable of how a chill wind forced a man to button his coat, but sunshine compelled him to remove it. Kim hoped to lure North Korea in from the cold with economic engagement and political summitry. In an unprecedented development, Hyundai built a tourist resort for South Koreans inside North Korea at the scenic Mount Kumgang. Subsequently, an industrial complex opened in Kaesong, north of Seoul across the DMZ, marrying the capital and expertise of Southern businesses with Northern labour – a blueprint for a possible Seoul-engineered economic revival of North Korea. Two inter-Korean summits were held, in 2000 and 2007, and DJ's peacemaking efforts won him a Nobel Peace Prize (subsequently devalued after it was revealed that he had secretly paid Pyongyang half a billion US dollars to enable his summit).

'Sunshine' was encouraging but, coinciding with the conservative George W. Bush administration, a policy

y

111

ALL THAT MATTERS: MODERN KOREA

disconnect opened between Seoul and Washington. In 2002 US officials confronted North Korea with intelligence concerning a secret, uranium-based nuclear arms programme. North Korea denied it. The troubled 'Agreed Framework' imploded, Pyongyang expelled nuclear inspectors and restarted Yongbyon. Concerned, Beijing took the initiative in 2003, sponsoring 'Six Party' denuclearization talks involving China, Japan, both Koreas, Russia and the United States. Negotiations proceeded uneasily and in 2006 Pyongyang upped the ante with an underground, plutonium-based nuclear test. Another followed in 2009. Talks finally collapsed in 2009 over disagreements on verification protocols for facility shutdowns. In 2010 Pyongyang revealed a uranium-based programme (overturning its 2002 denials); in 2012 it wrote nuclear power into its constitution and, in 2013, detonated a third device.

It was also conducting missile tests. In 2005 one flew over Japan and in 2013 a satellite was successfully launched. (Satellite launch vehicles are near-identical to ballistic missiles.) Pyongyang's progress in compressing fissile materials to warhead size, mastering re-entry technologies and engineering targeting systems is unknown, but, with major state resources being invested, it seems only a matter of time before North Korea is able to reach the United States with a nuclear payload. South Korea and Japan already lie inside attack radius. North Korea's 60,000-strong special units (the largest such force on earth) could feasibly load a nuclear device or 'dirty bomb' into a mini-submarine that could infiltrate

Tokyo Bay, or a disguised van that could be driven through a tunnel under the DMZ and parked in Seoul.

Strategic weapons give Pyongyang the deterrent muscle that its dilapidated army, now capable only of fast, pinprick strikes, has lost. They also provide a bargaining chip and grant an otherwise decrepit regime international relevance. And Pyongyang varies its messaging. It periodically requests a peace treaty with the United States (which Washington considers a ploy for the removal of the 28,000 US troops in South Korea). It also offers reunions of divided families to Seoul. (Some 22,000 persons have participated in 18 reunions since 1985; other planned reunions have been called off amid inter-Korean tensions.) By combining military threats and violent rhetoric with conciliatory gestures in an on-again, off-again negotiating cycle, Pyongyang plays a weak hand brilliantly. The Kims may be devious, but they are no lunatics.

The world has struck back with sanctions: broad US sanctions are problematic for all US firms planning business in North Korea, but EU and UN sanctions are precisely targeted on weapons trading and luxury goods. Against a regime prioritizing political power as primary, and public wellbeing and the economy as secondary, these sanctions have failed utterly to alter regime behaviour. Moreover, just as bombers found North Korea's countryside a 'target-poor environment' during the war, sanctions have little impact on a decimated economy. Nor have sanctions stopped China – irked by Pyongyang's dangerous behaviour but more worried by a potential regime collapse – funnelling investment, aid and trade across the Yalu. This raises fears in Seoul that North Korea is becoming a Chinese economic colony, particularly as North–South projects have sputtered. The Mount Kumgang tourist region closed in 2008 after a South Korean was shot dead by a North Korean soldier (an apparent accident). Investment in Kaesong appears to have peaked at 123 small firms; neither *chaebol* nor foreign investors seem keen to enter after North Korea pulled out workers for six months amid security tensions in 2013.

Meanwhile, Pyongyang undertakes a gamut of 'rogue state' activities. Having defaulted on some US$800 million of international loans in the 1990s, it stands accused of drug running, currency counterfeiting and even exporting nuclear technologies to Syria.

While few pundits anticipate a nuclear attack by Pyongyang – retaliation would annihilate the regime – the possibility of a vortex of escalation, from border clash to Armageddon, exists. Washington's nightmare is Pyongyang selling atomic assets to terrorists. Equally worrying (though less publicized) is safety. Yongbyon's graphite moderators present a huge fire risk, but there is no international oversight and sanctions curtail imports of safe, modern components. Yongbyon could become another Fukushima – perhaps with the outside world refused entry to undertake disaster management.

The situation is urgent. North Korea wants recognition, like Pakistan, as a nuclear state; having witnessed Libya's fate after it abandoned atomic arms, it has no intention of abandoning its current arsenal. But it could make concessions, such as programme freezes, in return for economic aid and diplomatic normalization. However, Seoul, Tokyo and Washington adamantly refuse nuclear status to North Korea. Thus all parties lie stranded in a perilously tight negotiating space.

Kims, kings and *chaebol*

If the Kims have established themselves as the new royalty of North Korea, who are their South Korean equivalents? Though Park II in Seoul faces Kim III in Pyongyang, the South Korean presidency is temporary, restricted to a single term. The real power holders in Seoul, unelected and dynastic, are the *chaebol* owner families, now passing power down to the third generation.

Mystique surrounds top-tier chairmen. They inhabit fortress-like compounds in exclusive, Seoul mountainside districts. They are rarely seen in public and conduct business behind closed doors. They are treated with reverence on the (rare) occasions when they meet employees. They are above the law – slapped wrists, suspended sentences and presidential pardons have been their customary 'punishment' for corporate crimes. They are above the media – they do not grant interviews. They are not answerable to shareholders – they do not attend AGMs. Their children (dubbed 'princes' and 'princesses' by the chattering class – they often intermarry) are raised to assume power and placed in key executive positions guided by trusted lieutenants. Praetorian guards of loyal executives help them control their listed companies (most have only minority stakes). Like the Kims, their key concern is power. Unlike the Kims, who have proved disastrous rulers, the chairmen have enriched those below them, for their companies have been tremendously successful.

What, then, of the original Joseon royalty? Disempowered in 1910, they were taken to Japan and intermarried with minor Japanese royalty. Yi Gu, the grandson of Gojeong, was born in Japan in 1931 and learned Japanese as his first language. After 1945 royal property was nationalized under Rhee, so Yi studied in the United States, became an architect and married an American, 'Princess Julia'. During the Park years, the couple relocated to Korea and moved into a small compound in the royal palace. But Yi's architectural skills were mediocre. He did not prosper; he divorced Julia and returned to Japan.

I interviewed Yi briefly during his annual visit to perform ancestral rites in Seoul in 2004. Attired in royal ceremonial silks, he was a small, sad-looking man, strongly resembling photos of Gojeong. A US passport holder, he said he considered himself Korean, and wished to be buried in Korea. I was the last reporter to interview him: he died the following year in Tokyo and was buried as per his wishes.

One man still hopes for restoration. Yi's cousin, Yi Seok, was deported from his palace as a child, became an entertainer, went to Vietnam and endured homelessness before being granted a traditional home in the city of Jeonju where he is a living tourist attraction. His dreams of restoration look slim. When I interviewed him in the palace grounds, local students asked to pose for pictures with me, a foreigner, but were totally uninterested in the man whose family home the palace once was.

6

Quo vadis, Korea?

*'Just as there are many
stars in a clear sky
There are many dreams
in our hearts.
There, over the hills, lies
Mount Baekdu
Where, even in midwinter,
flowers bloom ...'*

'Arirang', Korean folk song

In under half a century, South Korea overcame centuries of poverty as it industrialized, centuries of ill-governance as it democratized, and centuries of insularity as it globalized. This national success story is inspirational; to some developing nations, it is aspirational. Yet the country has not given birth to the perfect society.

Its economy is burdened by a hardware/software mismatch and by dubious and abusive corporate practices – holdovers from the era of rushed economic development. Wider society faces structural, institutional and cultural challenges stemming from a tangled combination of rushed development, the ˙palli palli˙ customs that the era spawned, and traditional culture.

▶ Economic imbalances

At first sight – or from afar – South Korea's economy, armed with its impressive quiver of world-beating brands and boasting an efficient, high-tech infrastructure, delivers a gobsmacking impression of success. But, below the surface, dark shadows loom.

South Korea's economy is lopsided: it boasts multiple world-class manufacturers but no world-class services firm. Originally, this related to policy: metal bashing was the national priority, not services. But there are other factors. Finance has never been fully unleashed, having operated so long under government control and heavy regulation: even today, Seoul influences appointments of top bank executives. Consulting has never been a major sector: *chaebol* prefer in-house teams. Legal services were so long protected – the market opened only in 2012 – that they boast local but neither regional nor global competitiveness. Leisure/tourism remains under-invested in, particularly for international tourists. Medical services (notably cosmetic treatments) offer potential, but the service that one might expect South Korea to be most competitive in – education – is hugely problematic.

The economy is also dangerously export-centric. With exports making up 54 per cent of GDP, South Korea is a slave to global growth, leaving the country's capital markets and currency vulnerable to external shocks. (Moreover, the won is not globally traded, which would lower volatility.) With South Korea suffering high household debt (135 per cent of GDP), domestic consumption cannot drive growth. And with national infrastructure largely in place and demand for apartments and offices having peaked, the potential of the customary domestic economic booster – construction – has dwindled.'

Above all, South Korea's economy is top-heavy: *chaebol* dominate capital and human resources. While there are innumerable small businesses in the country – mom-and-pop restaurants, shops, educational institutes, private taxis and so on (the descendants of the survival capitalists of the Korean War) – most are owner-operated, so risk-laden. Largely absent are entrepreneurial ventures and mid-sized companies that can form the next-generation top tier. Traditionally, all available monies flowed to *chaebol*, leaving other businesses undercapitalized. '[South] Korea is capitalism without capital!' says economics Professor Shin Se-don. The Park Geun-hye administration has poured huge amounts into start-up funds, but whether throwing money will solve the problem is unclear.

As for the *chaebol*, they are great companies, but in many ways unpleasant corporates. During their formative years, these locomotives of growth enjoyed the benefits of nationalized companies – projects, funding, protection – while remaining family businesses. But while many South Koreans take pride in the *chaebol*'s global success, their earnings were unevenly distributed. *Chaebol* 'royal families' became hugely enriched and, consequently, powerful. They tend not to be majority shareholders of their (publicly traded) companies, but control their empires through cross- and, more latterly, circular-shareholdings. In a culture where information has always been tightly held, managerial decision-making is opaque. *Chaebol* are non-responsive to shareholders and customarily pay low dividends. This, married to their opacity and the endless scandals of their unaccountable ruling families – involving embezzlement, fraud, slush funds, inheritance scams, tax evasion – explains the 'Korea Discount', under which global investors undervalue South Korean stocks relative to their competitors'. (Many local pundits insist that the risk posed by North

Korea underlies the discount. Foreign fund managers, speaking confidentially, differ.) Local critics allege that *chaebol* grant preferential 'inside' deals to their affiliates, abuse small companies, force them into submissive relationships, pay them late and even poach ideas, staff and technologies. Most corrosively, the endless misdemeanours of South Korea's business elite teach a damaging lesson to aspirational Koreans – that success requires criminality.

Chaebol power abuse has ignited anti-business sentiment in a nation enriched by a dirigiste, rather than a laissez-faire, economy. There is unease with capitalism, a system that successfully generates wealth but distributes it unevenly. This may be due to old, deeply embedded abuses: for example, there is minimal understanding of shareholder rights, but a huge sense of labour rights. 'Chinese are capitalist socialists, but Koreans are socialist capitalists!' lamented one retired *chaebol* family member, and South Koreans do, indeed, look to government for all answers. While modern South Koreans are intensely competitive, they also harbour apparently contradictory senses of equality and entitlement. (Economic data suggests that South Korea is reasonably egalitarian, but public perceptions are of accelerating economic polarization, which made welfare central to the 2012 election.) These mind-sets makes incentivization difficult. Standard Chartered Bank Korea sparked the country's longest banking sector strike after introducing performance-related pay.

▶ Structural flaws, institutional issues and cultural questions

In individualistic Western nations, the word 'culture' – that is, learned behaviour; 'nurture' rather than 'nature' – is rarely heard. In collective-spirited South Korea, however, the weight of culture is significant, overhanging institutions and social structures.

One reason that the *chaebol* have been able to get away with egregious power abuse is that the legal system has been kind. It has been customary for judges to give light or suspended sentences to convicted chairmen, 'because of their importance to the economy'. (This raises troubling questions. If judges believe this, why have they chosen justice rather than business as their profession? And given the opacity of Korean management, how can judges know whether chairmen are assets or liabilities to their companies? Tellingly, Samsung's stock price shot up in 2014 when news broke of its chairman's heart attack.) Courtroom theatrics are common, with some *chaebol* bosses ('wheel-chairmen') arriving in hospital pyjamas or on gurneys, to generate sympathy. Sentencing can be farcical. In 2008 a court found that Kim Seung-youn of Hanwha Group, South Korea's tenth largest *chaebol*, mobilized security guards and gangsters to kidnap bar workers who had ejected his son from a Gangnam watering hole. Kim then tortured them. Kim's hired thugs were jailed but the chairman himself escaped with 200 hours' community service. (Kim was jailed in 2012 for an unrelated embezzlement conviction.) In rare cases when chairmen are convicted, they often receive presidential pardons. The heads of the country's top three businesses – Samsung Electronics' Lee Keun-hee, Hyundai Motor's Chung Mong-koo and SK Corp's Chey Tae-won – have all been granted the latter. (At time of writing, Chey is serving his second jail term for embezzlement.)

Why are the insitutions of South Korea so kind to *chaebol* godfathers? Firstly, since the 1960s the country has hyper-prioritized its economy – with resultant favour to businessmen. Corruption may be another factor, but the best explanation may be that the Establishment – politicians, regulators, justices, business chiefs – looks after its own.

More broadly, the law has never been a popular institution. South Korea's legal system was imported from colonist Japan; then, and under the military dictatorships, it was a tool of abuse. And Koreans had always preferred to handle matters personally rather than through an impersonal and expensive institution. While, say, an American and a Briton who have never met can do a deal based on a signed contract, Koreans have customarily been uncomfortable with such arrangements, preferring to work with people they know or have a relationship with.

Relationships may regulate society more effectively than institutions. The networks of family, school, neighbourhood and so on may explain the happily low levels of street crime: unlike Western inner cities, 'no go' areas are absent in South Korea. Conversely, to witness South Koreans' disdain for the law (in a situation where no relationship hierarchies exist to order behaviour), observe road use. Red lights are run, buses are a menace, motorcycles race along pavements, and police do little. The country has excellent laws and competent legal professionals, but the law is abused, under-utilized and spottily enforced.

If an 'old boys network' explains why justice weighs so lightly on corporate South Korea, the reason big business gets an easy ride in the press is easier to explain. While the South Korean media freely covers almost every aspect of society (including politics) without restraint, business coverage is compromised: it is an open secret that *chaebol* wield their advertising budgets to influence coverage.

Another ally of big business has been the civil service. In Joseon, the elite were neither warriors nor merchants, but scholarly civil servants. This tradition was revived under Park Chung-hee: top civil servants planned the economic miracle, then oversaw its implementation. Alas, regulators got too close to business, which often paid them to overlook burdensome regulation. Collusion was a key factor behind the public safety disasters of the 1990s and the 1997 economic crisis. Oversight failures were likely a factor in the sinking of the overloaded ferry *Sewol* in April 2014, and for the loss of some 300 passengers, mostly high schoolers. The inefficiency and overlap of various government bodies in rescue and recovery operations, and the bureaucratization of procedures, infuriated the public and forced the resignation of the hapless prime minister. South Korea's prime minister is not elected, but is a presidential appointee who tends to be drawn from civil service or academia; a thinker rather than a doer. The *Sewol* tragedy showed that crisis leadership demands a man of action, not a paper shuffler.

South Korea's customary powerful bureaucratic control instinct is not weakening. Businesses beg for transparency and predictability, but complain of over-regulation, agency overlap, and regulations being drafted without consultation and implemented without warning. In 2014 President Park Geun-hye oversaw a seven-hour (!) meeting during which she ordered the bureaucratic mafia to slash the red tape strangling the country. But nanny statism remains rampant. For example, North Korean websites are firewalled, while tourists returning from overseas are searched to make sure that they have not overspent, indicating that the governing class is distrustful of the public. All this poses a broad question: is South Korea's civil service, formerly a national competency, becoming a national liability?

To shift focus from structures to culture, another issue wracking South Korean society is its ferocious competitiveness. This may date back to the insidious life of the peasantry – with its sense of 'If Kim has something new, Park and Lee want one, too' – but intensified amid surging development. It is visible on both the national – media overflow with stories reporting South Korea's rankings in every kind of international survey – and the personal – the competition to graduate from the best university, join the best company, live in the best sub-district of Gangnam, etc. – levels. Koreans' competitive dynamism is appropriately fuelled: there are probably more coffee shops crowding the country's cities than in any others on earth; the bouquet of roasting beans has overwhelmed the waft of *kimchi*. But while competitiveness is an asset for business, it creates a pressure-cooker society in which the underachiever is toast.

A Korean *ajumah* (matron) in New Maldon – the 'Koreatown' south of London – once told me that she loved British life for its 'freedom'. Though South Korea is no less democratic than the UK, she was talking not about political or legal freedoms, but social freedoms: liberation from the smothering influence of groupthink, social expectation and peer pressure. These pressures can be extreme, manifested in such ills as school and cyber bullying. Tellingly, one of the worst forms of bullying in this group-oriented society is *wanggta* (ostracism),

In a cruel irony, South Koreans have written one of the great national success stories of modern times, but surveys indicate that they are far from happy. South Koreans play as hard as they work, but during raucous nights out they often confide that they are recreating not for enjoyment but for stress relief. President Park Geun-hye made 'happiness' the central theme of her inaugural speech, but how she can achieve it is less clear; it will require social engineering more than policymaking.

The programmed urge to scramble to the top of the heap is widely analysed as being behind the spectacular fall of

Dr Hwang Woo-suk. A brilliant stem-cell scientist at the renowned Seoul National University, or SNU, he amazed the world with Snuppy ('SNU' plus 'puppy'), a cloned dog. Hwang was toasted as a hero burnishing South Korea's global image, but then came the bombshell: some of his research was falsified. An angry public turned. Disgraced, Hwang fled overseas.

Yet Hwang, a risk taker, was, in one sense, unusual: so harsh are South Korea's penalties for failure, that risk aversion is the norm. Venture entrepreneurs, if their businesses fail, find their credit history forever besmirched, meaning that they only get one chance; this explains why the country is not churning out Bill Gates or Steve Jobs. (And it would be virtually unthinkable for a Korean to drop out of an elite college to found a venture.) In offices, risk aversion is a feature of the suit-wearing class, hampering innovation and breeding second-, not first-, movers.

Intense competitiveness and by-the-book programming is most visible in education. Western parents enviously viewing South Korean children's international test scores may be astonished to learn not only how strongly South Koreans criticize their own education system, but also how much they invest in it.

Educational achievement was prized in Joseon but, in modern South Korea, has been elevated to a ridiculous extreme. Children routinely spend hours in *hakwon* (after-hours cram schools) or with tutors; high-school pupils study into the wee hours. The *hakwon* sector's estimated annual worth is US$18 billion. Educational expenses top family spending, teachers are exasperated that so many students are ahead of the curriculum, and parents recognize that childhoods are being whittled away – but still push them to study, endlessly.

Study is undertaken neither for personal interest nor betterment of character; it focuses on the 'destination' of test results or qualifications, rather than the 'journey' of knowledge or skill acquisition. Take English. South Koreans made huge efforts to learn it, but their curriculum is so test-centred that many are unable even to answer the telephone in the language. The problem persists in further education. A Japanese chef recalls how, after graduating from a culinary school in Italy, he decided to work in Italian kitchens for a couple of years to gain experience. But his Korean colleagues all flew home and, brandishing their new diplomas, immediately opened restaurants.

The all-important test is the university entrance exam. Many children who fail this test are sequestered in prison-style cram schools where, isolated from society, they are literally forced to study for next year's resit. But it is risky for any administration to tinker with this system: the university entrance exam is one area of South Korean life that is fair and corruption-free.

Despite the time, sweat and money South Koreans invest in education, the country's universities are mediocre: Seoul National, South Korea's top college, only managed 35th and 44th places in the two major global higher education surveys of 2013. Partly, this is due to pressure from students and parents to keep fees low: colleges cannot afford the best facilities or the best professors.

Another issue is the cushy lifetime tenure granted to academics: once hired, there was no pressure for them to research. However, there are grounds for optimism. Motivated South Korean professors are returning from top schools overseas armed with international best practices, and the numbers of foreign students, largely from Asia, are rising.

Still, due to what a Harvard educator calls South Korea's 'inhuman' education, there is a rush to escape. Hordes of the country's children travel abroad: in 2013 some 20,000 enlisted in overseas schools. Often, mothers accompany children, leaving Dad alone in Korea, working joylessly to remit money. Even greater numbers study in overseas universities, (seen as more prestigious than local ones). But the grimmest result of educational – and wider competitive and peer – pressures is a suicide epidemic. Suicide has overtaken traffic accidents as the biggest killer of South Koreans under 40; the country tops OECD suicide rates.

'Education mania' has contributed to a looming future problem: South Korea's rapidly greying society. As in other advanced nations, modern South Korean women want careers rather than children. Add to this the monetary burden of education costs, and the result has been a plummeting fertility rate. Working-age South Koreans peak in 2016; thence, the country faces a reduced workforce, shrunken tax base and increased welfare spend for the elderly.

Traditional reliance upon relationships and networks over institutions engenders, inevitably, nepotism, cronyism and corruption. Many South Koreans hoped the stringent measures taken following the traumatic 1997 financial crisis would clean up society and matters did, indeed, improve. Yet corruption – among businessmen, politicians and regulators – is a regular news item. In 2013 the country was ranked 46th globally by Transparency International's Corruption Perceptions survey – a poor score for the world's 15th largest economy.

As a neo-Confucian society, South Korea was customarily male-dominated and, although it elected North-east Asia's first female president in 2012, the glass ceiling remains low. (And, like Britain's Margaret Thatcher, Park is no paragon of feminism: in one of the rudest political comments of all time, a local academic declared: 'The only thing feminine about Park Geun-hye are her genitals!') While the country's women are emancipating themselves, they are grossly underrepresented in senior ranks in government and, most notably, business: research firm CEO Score found only 13 female CEOs among South Korea's 1,787 listed companies.

South Korean society remains hierarchically ordered, broadly conservative and group-centric. On the plus side, hierarchical rank structures enable swift management, conservatism cuts risk, and groupthink solidifies teams. But these factors simultaneously militate against independent 'outside-the-box' thinking. Meanwhile, the importance of not disturbing others' *nunchi* ('sensitivities') generates office politics and hampers productivity (as do the excessive hours Koreans work). Related habits include not questioning seniors and even of prioritizing the satisfaction of bosses over clients; the snivelling, boss-worshipping underling is a comedy staple.

Despite – or perhaps in reaction against – society's hierarchical ordering, there is an increasingly passionate disrespect for authority. This is partly understandable. South Koreans have endured authoritarian leaders and still suffer from non-accountable business leaders and dirty politicians. In the 2014 *Sewol* disaster, dire leadership was fully displayed: inept officers issued murderous orders for passengers to remain below; a craven captain abandoned ship without thought for his charges; and an owner-chairman disappeared, post-disaster. Yet it was the government, perceived as bungling and inefficient, that suffered the most venomous criticism. It seems that, under South Korea's social contract, government has been so strong and intrusive that the people now blame it even for things beyond its control.

Mindful of their vocal critics, South Korea's leaders veer towards populism, following rather than leading their public. Bureaucrats institute knee-jerk responses in response to press criticism ('the law of public opinion'): in the wake of the *Sewol* disaster, school trips were banned and the entire Coast Guard disbanded. (Its roles will be split between different government agencies – likely to increase, rather than improve, the bureaucratization of operations.) Presidents, limited to single, five-year terms, don't need to win votes and so are free to institute necessary and/or unpopular policies – but still court populism. Late in his term, Lee Myung-bak became the first Korean president to visit the east coast islet of Dokdo. Dokdo's ownership is disputed with Japan (which calls it Takeshima). The move won Lee some kudos at home, but raised Tokyo's diplomatic hackles. Subsequently, matters further deteriorated and 2014's Seoul–Tokyo relations are arguably worse than at any time since 1945.

▶ Anti-Japan, Pro-China

Korean nationalism emerged organically in response to Japanese aggression, then was institutionalized, strengthened and leveraged under the authoritarian governments. Today, despite South Korea's globalization, it remains a hair-trigger force impacting diplomatic, strategic and economic matters.

While anti-Americanism has waned since 2008, anti-Japanesism has waxed. Bar protests against diplomatic normalization in 1965, anti-Japanese sentiment was muted until South Korea's pivotal transformative decade, the 1990s. Then, the colonial-era central government building in central Seoul was demolished and the emotive 'comfort women' and Dokdo issues exploded across public consciousness.

South Korea's narrative, promulgated in local and global fora, is that Japan is responsible for appalling historical crimes that it refuses to admit to or compensate for. Japan shares some responsibility for this perception. Some revisionist politicians dispute Japanese guilt and visit Tokyo's Yasukuni, where a handful of war criminals are enshrined alongside Japan's millions of war dead.

But this picture is incomplete. Japan officially compensated South Korea in 1965. It has apologized approximately 50 times, including the landmark Kono (1993) and Murayama (1995) statements. And, in 1994, Tokyo established a public–private-sector fund to compensate individual comfort women, including a signed letter from the Japanese prime minister. Yet a dogged Korean belief persists that Japan is non-contrite.

Surviving comfort women refused the 1994 compensation, deeming it 'unofficial'. Koreans conflate the colonization of Korea (1910–45) with the Pacific War (1937–45), during which Tokyo's worst crimes, such as the rape of Nanjing and biological warfare, took place in China. Some Koreans even equate the comfort women with the Holocaust. While the recruitment (often coerced or forced) of girls to work in military brothels was a horrible, degrading crime, it seems disproportionate to compare it to industrialized genocide.

'Han' and historical perceptions entangle current affairs. Recalling Imperial Japan, South Koreans fear Japanese rearmament (ignoring Tokyo's democratic credentials). Although South Korea holds Dokdo, there is enormous anger every time Japan states its claim: Koreans refuse to concede that a dispute even exists, and insist that Japanese moves on Dokdo in 1905 prefigured colonization. The government, activists and Korean-Americans are even demanding the international community add the (Korea-preferred) nomenclature 'East Sea' to the term 'Sea of Japan' on global maps.

Washington, seeking to bind Seoul and Tokyo into a trilateral Northeast Asian alliance, is irked. On paper, South Korea and Japan are natural partners: fellow democracies sharing similar economies, cultures and lifestyles, and individual Koreans and Japanese get along famously. However, on the national level, emotion trumps rationality. To change current perceptions requires leadership, but no Korean wants to be dubbed 'pro-Japanese'; there is more capital in being anti.

Strikingly, many South Koreans who experienced colonialism are less anti-Japanese than today's generation. (This extends to President Park who, perhaps mindful of her pro-Japanese father, refuses to meet Japanese Prime Minister Shinzo Abe, despite repeated entreaties.) One elderly Korean offers an unpalatable analysis of Japan-bashing. 'Franco-Vietnamese relations and American–Vietnamese relations are good because Vietnam defeated them,' he says. 'But neither China nor Korea defeated Japan.' The implication: South Korea will be unsatisfied until it humiliates Japan in a PR war.

Nationalism is not exclusively political: US businesses have suffered economic nationalism. Private equity funds that acquired distressed Korean assets after the 1997 crisis were portrayed as asset strippers, although their deals actually added value. Worst hit was Lone Star, which acquired Korea Exchange Bank in 2003. A clever local NGO coined the term *mok-tui* ('eat and run', referencing a customer who dines in a restaurant, than bolts without paying) for the deal and Lone Star was attacked by local media, regulators, government and justices. A battered Lone Star exited South Korea (with profits) in 2011. The case, one investment advisor opined, had an impact on the country's reputation in global financial circles more than did North Korea's nuclear tests.

Yet disastrous Chinese investments in South Korea's Ssangyong Motors and Hydis LCD generated no public emotion. This signals an under-reported trend. China–South Korea trade overtook South Korea–US trade in 2004, and while South Koreans slam Washington and Tokyo, they are wary of Beijing – a rising nation they are drawing ever closer to.

China is South Korea's largest export and investment destination. Chinese firms are increasingly competing with Korean companies, Korean companies are investing heavily in their fast-growing neighbour, and Park Geun-hye has energetically prioritized Sino-South Korean ties. But while economic ties expand and Beijing shares Seoul's animosity toward Tokyo, it ignores Seoul's strategic and diplomatic concerns. Beijing established a 2014 air-defence identification zone over a Yellow Sea reef claimed by Seoul. It arrests North Korean defectors and dispatches them home, where they face harsh punishment, rather than offering them to Seoul. And Beijing pays lip service to Pyongyang's denuclearization, but employs neither economic nor political leverage to that end.

Seoul need not make an 'either-or' choice between Washington and Beijing, but its diplomats face a formidable task. Echoing the old 'shrimp between whales' proverb, they must walk a tightrope between two competing superpowers, while juggling opposed economic and strategic considerations.

The varied domestic and international issues above present significant challenges for South Korea. However, when set against the barriers of the preceding half-century, they are piffling: Koreans have surmounted more daunting barriers, and their capacity for change is a national strength. But there remains one mighty challenge – a challenge that simultaneously presents a tremendous opportunity.

▶ Status quo, Armageddon or reunification?

Chances are, when you awake tomorrow, North Korea will still exist. The disappearance of a nation is an unusual event – but so odd, so isolated and so defiant of historical trends is North Korea, that pundits have been anticipating exactly that since the 1990s. Yet Pyongyang endures.

Some parties favour the status quo. China benefits from a buffer state on its strategic north-east frontier, and from a rare regional ally that consistently gives Washington the finger. Many South Koreans want continuity, given the staggering costs of unification: the lowest figure commonly cited is US$50 billion for year one. Compared to German reunification, demographics are inauspicious. In 1999, 63.7 million West Germans absorbed 16 million East Germans; in 2014, 50 million South Koreans face 23 million North Koreans. Moreover, East Germany had, by Eastern European standards, a decent economy. By East Asian standards, North Korea is a basket case.

Conversely, Japan and the United States would happily see North Korea evaporate, as would many South Koreans. President Park noted in 2014 that unification would be 'hitting the jackpot'. Visiting international investors are often briefed by Seoul officials on reunification's sunny uplands. Such briefings overlook the fact that, due to single presidential terms, Seoul lacks a long-term unification plan. (Administrative offices manned by defectors do exist, but are less a shadow government, more defector community services.) Both Park and her predecessor, Lee, publicly raised unification in hopes of sparking debate among disinterested southerners, but talk of unification by absorption infuriates Pyongyang – making it less, not more likely. The 1998–2008 'Sunshine Policy' was designed to overcome distrust and gently bring the Koreas together, but, having failed, the two states today are as divided and suspicious as ever. And rosy briefings overlook the heart-stopping scenarios that might prompt pre-unification.

One is war. While chances of a North Korean invasion seem fantastical given Pyongyang's overall decrepitude, a border clash spiralling into de-control is nightmarishly feasible. Another is regime implosion, coup or even civil war, with nuclear weapons in the mix. Were chaos to ensue, intervention by China – hyper-sensitive to frontier insecurity – looks likely. Sources confide that Chinese and Americans have held working-level talks on North Korean collapse, but not at the policymaker level. Ergo, a danger exists of Chinese intervention forces clashing with South Korean–US troops inside North Korea – 1950, *redux*. Gradual opening and reform by Pyongyang, during which it gradually expands relations with Seoul, is the ideal scenario, but looks distant given Pyongyang's history of insulation, its reform resistance, and its likely vulnerability to real change.

Even so, if unification scenarios are worrying, short-term, they are promising, long-term. Peaceful Korean unification would create positive impacts, nationally, regionally and globally.

South Korea has been slipping down global GDP rankings – from 11th in 1997 to 15th today – as countries with bigger populations and resources climb the economic ladder. Reunification would provide a rejuvenating boost. The North offers natural resources, from gold to hydroelectric, and a low-cost workforce that could (at least, temporarily) be kept in situ by preserving the DMZ as a customs barrier. The North's untapped consumer market – the last in Asia – would be flung open. Its infrastructure, from roads to power grid, requires ground-up rebuilding; huge opportunities for *chaebol*. With defence spend reduced, local and international capital could be freed for investment. South Korea is a de facto island, severed from Eurasia proper by the North; unification would grant direct road, rail and pipeline access to the continent. While some South Koreans view North Korean defectors as yokels, socio-cultural integration might benefit both parties.

While Southerners ease Northerners into modern, global society, Northerners' public spirit might help Southerners refocus from competitiveness back to community.

Meanwhile, a strategic *casus belli* in North-east Asia would disappear. China, Korea and Japan would have better-than-ever reasons to bind themselves into an EU-style regional community, offering positive outcomes for a global economy that is increasingly turning east.

Will reunification occur tomorrow? Next year? In ten years? Never? It is impossible to predict. But a spirit of historical inevitability hovers over unification, and Korea has a record of surprising the world. Were it to occur peacefully, a historic injustice would be undone; 23 million humans would be welcomed into the global family; and a gifted nation would at last be able to fulfil its potential and pursue its destiny as one people.

This 100 ideas section gives ways you can explore the subject in more depth. It's much more than just the usual reading list.

100 IDEAS

Ten sites to surf

1 http://english.yonhapnews.co.kr   Semi-official wire service delivering up-to-the-minute Korean news.

2 http://www.rjkoehler.com Contentious debate on all things Korea from a well-informed, highly opinionated blog-ship.

3 http://38north.org/ For policy wonks, probably the top website on North Korea.

4 http://www.dailynk.com/english   Online   newspaper staffed by (among others) North Korean defectors who maintain sources north of the DMZ.

5 http://www.seriworld.org Information, data and articles on Korean economic and business developments from Samsung Economic Research Institute.

6 http://english.visitkorea.or.kr/enu/index.kto If you are visiting Korea, the Korean Tourist Organization website gives you info on what's on, travel, things to do, places to stay and so on.

7 http://www.eatyourkimchi.com/ Love-it-or-hate-it but phenomenally popular site covering K-youth, K-pop and K-life.

8 http://zenkimchi.com/ Excellent food blog on Korea. Recipes, restaurants reviews and features – a cyber feast.

9 http://rjkoehler.tumblr.com/ Gorgeous Korea pictures from blogger Robert Koehler.

10 http://askakorean.blogspot.kr/ If this book does not answer all your Korea questions, ask what you need to here.

Ten books on South Korea

11 Mark Clifford, *Troubled Tiger: Businessmen, Bureaucrats and Generals in South Korea* Surprisingly compelling, warts-and-all account of the economic miracle.

12 Michael Breen, *The Koreans: Who They Are, What They Want, Where Their Future Lies* Infotaining explication of Korea by a long-term expatriate.

13 Daniel Tudor, *Korea: The Impossible Nation* Up-to-date, accessible introduction to Korea by another expatriate.

14 Bruce Cumings, *Korea's Place in the Sun* Engaging and accessible biography of modern Korea by a leading US historian.

15 Simon Winchester, *Korea: A Walk through the Land of Miracles* A journalist's travelogue in the early days of the economic miracle.

16 Choe Sangon-hoon, *How Koreans Talk* Fascinating examination of Koreans through the prism of their language.

17 Don Kirk and Choe Sang-hoon (eds), *Korea Witness* Korea's traumatic recent history, as experienced by the Seoul Foreign Correspondents' Club

18 Krys Lee, *Drifting House* Literate collection of short stories on the bitterness underlying modern Korean life in the South, the North and US Koreatowns.

19 Shin Kyung-sook, *Please Look after Mother* International bestselling novel covers the wrenching inner and outer struggles of a Korean family as they search for their troubled, missing matriarch.

20 Kim Young-ha, *Your Republic is Calling You* Thriller examining the dilemmas faced by a long-term North Korean sleeper agent in South Korea when he is unexpectedly activated.

Ten books on the Korean War / North Korea

21 Allan Millet, *The War for Korea* Magisterial, up-to-date, three-volume set (the last volume is pending publication) by the war's leading historian. The best history for the specialist.

22 Max Hastings, *The Korean War* Dated and Anglocentric, but balanced, comprehensive and superbly written. The best history for the general reader.

23 Andrew Salmon, *To the Last Round* By this author: the soldier's-eye view of combat, told by survivors of a tragic last stand that took place at the epicentre of the biggest communist offensive of the war.

24 Charles Hanley, Choe Sang-hoon and Martha Mendoza, *The Bridge at Nogun-ri* Pulitzer Prize-winning account of a Korean War atrocity.

25 Suh Ji-moon, *Brother Enemy: Poems of the Korean War* Many believe that the Korean War spawned no great literature. This moving translation of Korean poems demolishes that contention.

26 **Brian Myers,** *The Cleanest Race* Iconoclastic, influential book that overturned conventional wisdom and redefined North Korea by focusing on what its propaganda says about the nation.

27 **Andrei Lankov,** *The Real North Korea* Up-close, inside look at North Korea by arguably the world's leading expert on the state.

28 **Barbara Demick,** *Nothing to Envy* Prize-winning, fascinating biography of a North Korean town.

29 **Blaine Harden,** *Escape from Camp 14: One Man's Remarkable Odyssey from North Korea to Freedom in the West* Terse account of Shin Dong-hyuk, who was born in and escaped from one of the worst places on earth.

30 **Bradley Martin, Under the Loving Care of the Fatherly Leader** Massive tome on North Korea and Kims I and II by a leading journalist and expert on the state.

Ten Korean films to watch

31 *Seopyeonjae* (1993) Gorgeously shot saga of a family of troubadours struggling to adapt to a changing nation; features a breathtakingly cruel, 'only-in-Korea' plot twist. It sparked a national revival of Korean traditional music.

32 *JSA* (2000) Plot-centric thriller about a doomed friendship between North and South Korean troops, set in the infamous Joint Security Area in the DMZ.

33 *Old Boy* (2003) No introduction needed: brutal noir thriller that is a cult classic among those (like fan Quentin Tarantino) with a taste for the reddest cinematic meat.

34 *A Tale of Two Sisters* (2003) Edge-of-seat psychological horror film about two sisters and – maybe? – ghosts.

35 *Memories of Murder* (2003) Surprisingly contemplative serial murder drama based on true events that occurred during the last years of authoritarian rule.

36 *Taekugki* (2004) Brother-versus-brother in a searing Korean War epic made with Hollywood-style production values.

37 *The Host* (2006) Horror/black comedy/drama explores family, politics, pollution, the Korea–United States alliance… and a gigantic, man-eating eel.

38 *The Chaser* (2008) Tense thriller as a corrupt cop-turned-pimp belatedly realizes that his prize call girl has fallen into the hands of a serial killer.

39 *Crossing* (2008) Wrenching, but surprisingly little-known, South Korean tragedy about a North Korean defector's attempts to bring his family to the South. Based on a true story.

40 *Inchon!* (1981) Extravagantly funded by the Unification Church, this woeful flick was the most expensive flop in movie history. Laurence Olivier plays MacArthur as he plots the Incheon landing. So bad it's good – well, almost.

Ten Korean bands and musicians to listen to

41 Psy Even if he never releases another tune, the chubby prankster-rapper will forever be Gangnam's favourite son.

42 Busker Busker Folky, poppy threesome.

43 Big Bang One of the catchiest and least manufactured of K-pop boy bands.

44 H.O.T The lads whose performances led to the media coining the term 'Korean Wave'.

45 Crying Nut Good-natured crew whose catchy anthems define Korean punk.

46 **Seo Taeji** Acclaimed both as a musical genius and the godfather of K-pop.

47 **Cho Yong-pil** Classic crooner and Korea's equivalent of Tom Jones or Frank Sinatra, but still bang up to date.

48 **Hwang Byeong-ki** Master of the *gayageum*, Korea's zither; his contemplative twanging is uniquely Korean.

49 **Kim Young-dong** Fusion musician blends Korean and foreign sounds. His landmark album, *Sori Yohaeng* ('Travelling of Sound'), is one of the loveliest pieces of music created anywhere.

50 **Dulsori** Energetic, neo-traditional band and a firm favourite at WOMAD festivals.

Ten Korean foods and drinks to sample

51 *Galbi* Pork or beef ribs grilled on your tabletop barbecue. Definitive Korean feast.

52 *Samkyeopsal* Bacon-style pork belly, grilled and dipped in salt and sesame oil; the classic working man's dish.

53 *Bibimbap* Popular, simple hash of rice, veggies, meat, spicy sauce, an egg and – *voilà!*

54 *Doenjang jiggae* This stew is the strong, heavy (and original) version of Japan's miso, based on Korea's superb fermented soy-bean paste

55 *Kimchi jiggae* Close cousin of the above; stewed *kimchi* (fermented vegetables) with fish or meat added to the stew.

56 *Hanjonshik* Formal, *table d'hôte*-style set meal of Korea's vanished aristocracy.

57 *Pajeon* Hearty pancakes, usually including seafood or vegetables.

58 *Makgeolli* Unique, white tipple sometimes called rice wine but actually rice ale, this is the true taste of Korea. Hundreds of varietals are sold nationwide.

59 Dried squid Tasty but oh-so-chewy street snack, dipped in mayo or chili sauce.

60 *Boshintang* Dog lovers may be interested in savouring this thick, sesame-flavoured stew.

Ten places to visit in Seoul

61 Hongik University Artsy but unpretentious youth-focused food, drink and nightlife district; defines Kool Korea.

62 Namdaemun/Myeong Dong Respectively, Seoul's traditional and modern shopping meccas: a raucous traditional market adjacent to trendy shopping boutiques and department stores.

63 Palkgakjeong Lookout at the summit of Seoul's highest mountain suspended above downtown. The winding alpine roads leading to it are an attraction in themselves.

64 Cheongdam Dong/Apgujeong In deepest Gangnam, this area – 'Korea's Beverly Hills' – is all branded stores, palatial restaurants and terminal fashion victims.

65 Samcheong Dong Low-rise, pretty and romance-friendly district of boutiques, eateries and drinkeries, some in converted hanok (traditional cottages).

66 Gyeongbokgung The biggest and oldest of Seoul's medieval palaces, spectacularly sited and lovingly over-restored.

67 Seoul City Museum The story of the city told in a futuristic, gallery-like museum.

68 National War Memorial Massive museum showcases centuries of Korean martial history, with a strong emphasis on the Korean War.

69 **Kooksadang** Fascinating and photogenic clutch of tiny Buddhist temples clustered around the national shamans' shrine on the slopes of Mount Inwhang.

70 **Yeouido Park / Riverside Park** Fine walks, bike trails and views on the Han River island that is home to the National Assembly, broadcasting firms and the finance industry.

Ten places to go outside Seoul

71 **Chorwon** From a DMZ army observation post, gaze out over heartbreakingly beautiful countryside into North Korea (Seoul day trip).

72 **Gangwha Island** History-laden island dominating the Han River estuary. Fine temples, sea views, fortresses and prospects over North Korea (Seoul day trip).

73 **Songdo** For a glimpse into the towns of tomorrow, visit this high-tech, green-friendly settlement, built on a reclaimed island off the port of Incheon (Seoul day trip).

74 **Mount Seorak National Park** Korea's most famously scenic mountain range, perched on the east coast.

75 **Jeju Island** Voted one of the 'Seven Natural Wonders of the World', Jeju is overhyped but is still a hauntingly attractive, subtropical island – especially in the off-season.

76 **Pulkugsa** Korea's most famous Buddhist temple.

77 **Gyeongju** Pleasingly slow-paced, the capital of Silla is packed with remnants – tombs, temples, ruins – of the vanished kingdom.

78 **Busan** Korea's second city is almost as lively as Seoul, but with beaches.

79 **Ulsan** The Korean miracle up close: this is 'Hyundai Town', home not only to automotive plants but also the awesome Hyundai shipyard – the world's biggest.

80 Pyongyang Yes, it is increasingly easy to visit the Kimdom's capital. An untypical but fascinating holiday for those interested in current affairs – and great dinner-party conversation once you return home.

Ten things to buy and do

81 Lacquerware Pleasing gift items that are appropriate for home or office.

82 Celadon If you possess a durable credit card, Korean pottery is among the world's finest.

83 Dried seaweed Vacuum-packed snack makes a perfect accompaniment to beer.

84 *Jang* Invest in a jar of *gochujang* (fermented bean paste) or *doengjang* (fermented bean paste): it makes an excellent dip, sauce, stew/gravy thickener, cheese accompaniment or even pizza topping.

85 Modern *hanbok* The updated version of traditional dress makes comfy home/garden wear.

86 Get booted and suited. Twenty-first-century Koreans are regional trendsetters. For affordable-but-cool threads, head to Seoul's Dongdaemun area; for high-end brands, try Cheongdam

87 Get a nip and a tuck . Gangnam is the global epicentre for cosmetic surgery, so why not leave Korea looking prettier than when you entered?

88 Visit a *jimjilbang.* Uni-sex sauna complexes are perfect spots to de-stress and rejuvenate.

89 See a non-verbal show. *Nanta* ('Cookin'') is the most famous of these 'Stomp'-like shows, but there are plenty of other members of this funky genre that bypasses the language barrier.

90 Take a hike. Hills and mountains are ubiquitous and vertical terrain is where Koreans are at their most affable.

Ten business trip preparation tips

91 Learn a phrase or two of Korean. Even if you mangle the pronunciation, your hosts will appreciate the effort.

92 Ready a cache of business cards. These make your critical first impression.

93 Obtain the full names of your contacts. While Koreans often use initials or adopt a Western name with foreigners, these may not be used among Koreans themselves. If you ask for 'Johnny Kim' or 'JK', the receptionist may go blank.

94 Dress formally. Suits are de rigueur (though ties are sometimes optional).

95 Out with the old. Ensure that all gear – wallet, briefcase, gadgetry – is up to date. Koreans don't get the 'old and worn' look; old hat can be bad form.

96 Prepare presentable and odour-free socks. If your hosts take you to a good restaurant, you may be required to doff footwear.

97 Practise using both hands – to shake hands, to pour drinks and to give/receive business cards. One hand: casual. Two hands: respect.

98 In Seoul, ensure that your hotel is convenient to your meeting locations. If your contacts are north of the river and your hotel is in Gangnam, you will spend hours in traffic.

99 Clear your schedule for *après* **business** After-hours relationship building is critical.

100 Prepare a song for the *noraebang* **(karaoke salon).** You don't want to be a bad sport and pass the mic.

Index

Acknowledgements

The author and publisher would like to express their thanks for permission to use the following images: **Chapter 1:** South Korean soldiers © Keystone-France/Gamma-Keystone via Getty Images; **Chapter 2:** Hyundai Shipyard, Ulsan © Rex Features/Sipa Press; **Chapter 3:** The dying Lee-han Yeol © Rex Features/Canadian Press; **Chapter 5:** Kim Jong-il © REX/KeystoneUSA-ZUMA

Acknowledgements